The World of Angling

THE WORLD OF ANGLING

Edited by... Richard Wills

CONTRIBUTORS

DEREK FLETCHER   JOHN GODDARD   FRANK GUTTFIELD

WINSTON HALL   JACK HILTON

JOHN INGHAM   BILL KEAL   BILLY LANE

JOHN NEVILLE   JOHN PIPER

PETER TOMBLESON   PETER WHEAT   GWYN WILLIAMS

TOM WILLIAMS   COLIN WILLOCK

SOUVENIR PRESS LTD - LONDON

First published by Souvenir Press Ltd., London, W.1, and
simultaneously in Canada by The Ryerson Press, Toronto, 2.

SBN. 285. 50246. 8

Made and printed in Great Britain by
Gilmour & Dean Ltd., Hamilton and London.

CONTENTS

MEET THE 'THROW-AWAY' GIRL

Twenty-one-year-old Susan Campbell threw awa[y] a whopper and can still smile. Read about o[ur] Scarface the pike on Page 65.

LIST OF ILLUSTRATIONS

INTRODUCING...

The World of Angling

by Richard Wills, the Editor

A SHREWD observer of the Northern match-fishing scene once gave it as his opinion that if the steelworkers of Sheffield were permanently deprived of their weekly body-and-soul-reviving excursions to the great fishing centres in the Midlands and East Anglia, they would probably shrivel up and die.

At the other end of the industrial scale, I once met the wealthy owner of a coffee plantation in East Africa who commuted by jet twice a week from London to the plantation and relieved the strain by enjoying his salmon and trout fishing in between.

I have also encountered a number of men, self-employed or wage-earners, who have deliberately chosen jobs or professions which presumably provide enough money for their needs—and certainly the amount of time they want to spend on going fishing.

Whatever the reasons that draw so many hundreds of thousands to the rivers, lakes, canals and seas every weekend, it is clear that the attraction is so powerful that time, distance and other minor inconveniences, such as earning a living, are merely the hurdles to be cleared between one fishing trip and the next!

To them, and the rising generation of anglers in whose hands the makers of fishing tackle place every year more sophisticated and better equipment, this book is happily dedicated. For this is a big name book of fishing, the big names of the present generations whose personalities and great affection for the sport come through so strongly as truly representative of THE WORLD OF ANGLING.

PIKE... the most rewarding fish of all

BY
BILL KEAL

Newspaperman, big-fish hunter and, above all, a dedicated, self-less angler, Bill Keal has achieved a considerable reputation for his consistent successes in carp and pike fishing. He is also secretary of the exclusive Red Spinners Angling Society, one of Britain's oldest angling organisations.

IN my view fishing for pike is perhaps the most rewarding branch of angling. The fish are big. They are in most lakes and rivers, and most days they will happily clamp their great jaws on any bait you care to offer.

Besides, a pike angler can tackle his sport in so many ways. A specialist may have up to a dozen rods for handling one particular method. But, truly, anyone can manage pike fishing perfectly well with a single rod. It is where the bait is cast and what the angler makes it do that really counts.

Most pike-men have a favourite way of setting out after their fish, but the expert will usually decide on the day just what method of fishing he will adopt.

On a summery sort of day with a good stiff breeze, when pike have appetites like tropical sharks, the expert will go spinning with big, flashy but lightweight spoons. He will go at it with a boat if he can, but the bank will suit him almost as well.

He will cast his spoon wherever he sees rushes and weed-beds, for that is where the pike lie, camouflaged and watchful for unsuspecting prey. No matter if the weed comes almost to the surface and threatens to tangle the spoon before it has travelled

Most people think of pike as winter fish, but just as many just as big can be caught in the summer. How about this Keal capture, for example? All of 29lb 14oz.

Bill Keal with a magnificent winter pike, weighing 29lb 12oz. He captured this specimen when the ground was iron hard with frost. Winter 'piking' is great sport for hard-weather enthusiasts.

a foot. For if weed is where the pike are, then it is pointless to cast the lure elsewhere.

To avoid the tangle, simply hold the rod high and jerk the spoon back at high speed so that it flips this way and that through the wave-tops. When they see it, pike go mad and lash out in fury, smashing their way to the surface and often coming clean out of the water in a frantic effort to prevent a meal from slipping away.

You only have to catch one pike that way to know why men go spinning. But wait. There are other ways. . . .

On that same summery day, as evening comes and the breeze drops to leave the water oily calm, dimpled here and there by flitting insects and feeding fry, you will often see the expert change his flashing spoon for a plug bait that floats. These usually have a built-in action which makes them wobble, flip and scurry, like some startled dabchick or frog, simply by reeling in at a slow, easy pace.

Plug baits work only when the water is calm, and they are best in the evening, cast across those same weed-beds. Pike cannot resist them; they come exploding from the depths of their weedy lairs the moment they detect the little surface splashes of the lure.

Spinning and plug fishing work rather less well on coldish days, when pike tend to be a little lethargic. They would rather lie in wait and sidle out to seize their prey. Those are the days to tempt them with a dead fish, cast out and slowly retrieved, lowering and raising the rod point all the while, so that the bait rises and falls rather like a dying fish might do in its last erratic moments.

This has a special appeal to the killer instinct of the pike, especially on those cold days when it is unable to get off the mark quite so quickly.

If there is weed about always work the dead-bait alongside or even among the beds. Where the weed is very dense, the bait should be drawn across the top of them with a jerking action of the rod.

This causes the bait to skim first one way and then another – not so much like a dying fish but more the action of an uncertain lamb separated from its mother! And as it moves rather faster through the water, but sinks less slowly than a spoon, it can be worked at a correspondingly slower pace better to suit the mood of the pike.

On the chilliest of all days, when the ground underfoot is frost hard and every breath shows on the air, the expert resorts to live-baiting or legering with a dead-bait. For this is when pike are at their most cussed, to match the weather.

They will feed, but they need to be tempted. So put all your skill and experience into finding them and casting your bait to them.

As a rule the pike will pay no attention, and if the live-bait on the line notes the danger and swims away within the limits of your line, the pike will usually let it go. But if that bait is made to stay, the pike, sooner or later, will find the temptation too great to bear and help himself. A legered dead-bait, which is simply cast into the swim and left there, is successful under those conditions for exactly the same reason.

As for the places where an expert will search for pike these are reed fringes and bays. Weed-beds will have mostly died down with the coming of the frosts, so the search must be among the other lairs

On the chilliest of all days, pike are at their most cussed to match the weather. Tempt them, says Keal.

and hidey-holes.

These may be in the shadow of steep banks, deep holes in the lake bed, behind rock piles, amid the roots of sunken trees—anywhere that may provide shelter. In rivers, undercut banks, eddies, the tail-ends of rush beds are the spots the expert first searches.

Always he searches. Some days he will take a dozen fish, often only a couple. Rarely will he take none.

His pike may be mere striplings of a few pounds. On a good day, at least one or two of his fish will be 10lb or 12lb, perhaps 16lb or 17lb. On an exceptional day, his prize will top 20lb – that's three-and-a-half feet of fighting fury, with a mouth big enough to put your arm in and teeth as long and a dozen times sharper than a dog's chewing equipment. Great sport, this pike fishing!

Winter or summer, the search for pike goes on . . . among reed fringes and bays. You seek him anywhere that may provide shelter, says Bill Keal.

SHORE FISHING, BEACH CASTING, PIER and ROCK FISHING

THOUSANDS of anglers fish from the shore all the year round—and they catch many different species. In the north the cod and codling predominate, while southern anglers prefer to concentrate on bass, a fish noted for its fighting ability.

But in all areas there are many other fish which can be caught from the beach. Of course, it does depend on the locality but one can expect plaice, sole, flounders, whiting, mackerel, conger, and even tope and skate from some deep, shelving shores.

From estuary marks, and land-based spots in harbours, the variety which can be creeled is often greater. Add such species as grey mullet, pollack, silver eels and garfish to those I have listed.

For general, straightforward beach fishing it is best to keep the business end of your tackle as uncomplicated as possible. The single hook flowing trace, fished leger style, is far better than gear with several hooks.

Most newcomers to sea angling believe bigger catches are possible with every additional hook which is added. This is a fallacy. Once experience is gained, greater creels will result with one-hook gear. This is because the bait can move around in the surf in a more natural manner, and striking is

by Derek Fletcher

Derek Fletcher — author, broadcaster and columnist in the 'Daily Telegraph' and 'Sunday Telegraph' — has fished all around the coastline of the British Isles and in major foreign salt-water festivals. He lives on the Hampshire coast, close to Christchurch, where he fishes from pier, shore and boat.

GROYNE, PIER
and HARBOUR WALL...

also easier. Certainly, casting will improve when the terminal tackle is kept to a minimum.

It is important to use a fibre-glass rod of a fairly good length, certainly not less than 10ft. With short rods, the surf movement hitting the line will soon force the tackle back to your feet.

There are many reels on the market for shore work, and it is wise to set aside as much money as possible for this item of equipment. If you have angling friends, try out their reels first to find the one most suited to you.

Multiplier and fixed-spool reels are both popular, but fixed-spool reels are easier to master at the start. Many anglers use centre-pin reels, and there is also a version which allows you to cast with a

fixed-spool style and then revert back to centre-pin fishing. Whatever reel is chosen, they all need plenty of casting practice to become proficient.

To become a constantly successful shore fisherman, it is important to learn everything about your particular seabed. There are favourite spots where fish are more likely to be caught . . . places where tasty titbits of food will be washed into gullies, and eagerly sought by many species.

Spy out a new beach at low-water so as to pinpoint likely-looking spots worth casting when the tide makes. At the same time you can dig for ragworm or lugworm, or collect shellfish for bait. Strips of herring or mackerel, cut about six inches long, also make useful baits at times, although after

Many and varied are the fish caught from piers up and down the country—and many and varied are the vantage points from which the line is cast. A popular spot with Brighton anglers is the Groyne by the Palace Pier (extreme left);

Bournemouth visitors of all ages settle for the pier (centre picture); and we would like to think the lone angler (above) on the harbour wall at Scarborough reaped his reward.

casting one needs to keep them moving for best results.

It is always better to hold the rod than to prop it up on a rod stand after casting. This way, the bite can be felt and struck accordingly.

When pier fishing it is equally important to know the type of bottom being fished, and this knowledge often decides the best method.

Pier anglers can leger with tackle similar to beach work, or they can use a lighter set of tackle and fish with a float. These complete changes of tackle come with experience—and, naturally enough, the desire to own more than one rod and to fish in different ways will come when the 'apprenticeship' stage is over.

Most piers have good and bad areas. The most productive spots usually benefit from an accumulation of broken shellfish moved into position by the tidal flow. Or maybe a feeding spot has been set up by food scraps thrown overboard daily from a pier cafe.

Many pier anglers, when they start, make the mistake of over-casting the fish. The best technique is to work around the weed-covered piles, for here is where many fish nose around for food.

A wide variety of fish are caught from piers all over the country, but it is fair to say the majority belong to the flatfish family, particularly flounders and plaice. These are caught with legered bait, but a more sporting method is to use a float, allowing the chosen bait to trip just over the seabed.

Yet another pier-fishing technique is known as the lifting method. The line runs unknotted from the reel to the hook and the system is to keep the bait on the move by lifting action around the piles. The rod-tip is raised every few seconds and bass or pollack under the ironwork will find it hard to resist. Be sure the bait goes in quietly, without a splash that will frighten off the fish.

More fish are caught from piers at night, particularly if there is good illumination. Small fish and other sea life move towards light attraction and the larger feeding fish quickly follow up. Float-fishing is very useful after dark, as fish tend to rise at night, although rougher or colder weather conditions may keep them at a deeper depth.

Many of the large mullet landed every year come

from rocky coastlines. Bass are also good sport among the rocks, and there are pollack, wrasse, codling and many other visitors. It is also surprising just how many fair-sized conger will move into a quiet, rocky area.

The best method of catching fish from rock stations is with float tackle, but bottom gear can be used if one does not mind the occasional loss through snagging on submerged rocks or heavy concentrations of weed, which often attract the fish. It is believed that seaweed is a sort of medicine for certain species.

There is much wrong thinking about rock fishing. One does not have to get soaking wet from pounding waves for the best results. In such conditions it is better to stay at home! An ideal situation is calmer conditions, with a gentle spray

Beach casting on a North Wales storm beach at the turn of the tide.

washing the rocks–and any minute sea life with it.

Gentle surf will attract most rock-swimming fish, especially bass, in the late evening where foam bubbles in the rocky inlets. Both pollack and mullet are similarly attracted, particularly if good groundbait is added.

It is pointless sprinkling in groundbait that is likely to be swept away by fast tides. So the chosen mixture needs putting into paper bags, weighted with sand or a stone. These soon burst on the bottom, scattering the contents around the rocks and crevices.

Many anglers have their own pet groundbait mixtures, and it is best to experiment until the most attractive mix is found for one's area.

This could be boiled rice flavoured with pilchard oil, pounded crabs or mussels, shrimps, bread or ragworm and lugworm cut into small pieces. Alternatively, chopped herring or mackerel spread over the rocks is good. The pieces are carried into the sea by the surf action.

For general float-fishing around rocks, the ideal is a light 10ft rod with a smart pick-up action, balanced by a small, free-running centre-pin reel. The line should be about 8lb, with a trace of lower breaking-strain. It is best to use a sliding float when rocks are surrounded by a good depth of water, because the peg-type hinder recovery by jamming at the rod tip.

Numerous baits can be used, and it is usually the ones that fish expect to find there that are most successful. These include prawns, shrimps, soft and peeler crabs. Live sandeels are also good.

Rock-caught fish will often vary in their fighting tactics, compared with those caught in the open sea. Instead of long runs, they head straight for the bottom in an attempt to smash the tackle. All fish must be made to fight it out on the surface, for if they reach the sanctuary of submerged rocks, the chances of landing them are lessened.

Also try experimenting around rocks with feathered lures worked on a trace from a roving float. Best results are likely in calm seas, and twilight is a productive time.

Hooks? It is wise to err on the smaller size. Obviously, commonsense is called for, and the size or type of bait being used is an important consideration. But always buy good-quality hooks.

And while at the tackle shop, don't forget a good-sized net to help land those rock-caught specimens.

Practice all the time is essential, says Derek Fletcher. Here is a good example of a rapid run-up with the rod well back. The left foot is still in the air as the cast is about to start.

On the rocks...

Yorkshire anglers using traditional East Coast rock fishing gear. On the left, a fine action study of a lone angler casting from a grassy slope on top of Flamborough Cliffs; below, the scene fifteen miles farther North, at Red Cliffe, Cayton Bay, haunt of the Scarborough Rock Anglers.

Sunny days by the seaside...

And when the sun is shining, there is no finer place on earth than the South Coast, says many a London angler. No matter whether you prefer the sandy beaches near Boscombe Pier (above) and Southbourne (bottom picture), or the surf and pebbles of bracing Sussex at Worthing (left) and Hastings (below).

...wish you were here!

MY QUEST FOR BARBEL

BY GWYN WILLIAMS

GWYN WILLIAMS began fishing in the mountain streams of Wales for trout, but soon graduated to bigger waters and other fish. He took pike to 25lb, chub to 5¾lb and tench to just under 6lb. Now, schoolmaster Gwyn lives in Luton and specialises in barbel fishing. In each of the last six seasons, he has caught at least one double-figure fish –his best a superb 12lb 11oz.

THE first symptoms of my annual attack of 'barbel fever' appear when rivers become clear enough and warm enough for these unpredictable fish to be located. This malaise takes a stronger grip during the summer period of low-water fishing and is at its most intense in autumn when the quest for specimen barbel really begins in earnest.

The task of location begins in May when barbel are spawning. For this purpose, they congregate in large shoals where the gravelly shallows deepen into the pools below.

At first, the only fish to be seen are a shoal of chub as they lie nose to tail near the surface of the pool, but if one's eyes are allowed to search long and deep, a huge orange fin will appear and gradually the bronze, bulky shape of a barbel will materialise around it. It will seldom be alone, and soon others will be seen as they twist and turn in the current.

When a shoal of barbel has been located, I examine all the likely swims in the area. If at any point the main current undercuts the bank, barbel are likely to be found there later in the season, especially if a tree overhangs the water. I look for deeper pockets of water sheltered by beds of bulrushes and for channels in the river bed which, as summer progresses, become hidden under a frond of waving weed.

I pay particular attention to shallows adjacent

to these swims, and ledges and depressions are marked down as the hot spots from which barbel will pick up a bait. Beds of underwater lilies often grow in profusion on these shallows and, although barbel avoid all other forms of vegetation during the hours of darkness, they will sometimes root for food in the middle of these cabbage patches, vacating them only when daylight makes their presence conspicuous.

Where to fish when the season opens is largely determined by river conditions. If the summer has been a wet one and rivers are high, I take advantage of the opportunity and fish in swims that I know to contain barbel of specimen size. On the other hand, if the rivers are low, which is more often the case in June, I fish during the summer for small barbel.

Some swims hold large numbers of these fish. Most of them weigh between 1lb and 3lb, but they provide good sport in spite of their lack of weight and, what's more, they are fairly easy to catch.

On a warm, sultry evening, the shallows will often be alive with these small barbel and the best approach is to leger for them using sausage meat or cheese paste as bait. A size 8 hook should be tied to a 5lb monofilament line, with a link-leger made up of swan shot stopped one foot from the hook.

On a favourable evening, sport will be fast and furious and even when it is not, these barbel can sometimes be induced to pick up the bait if it is moved every so often. To achieve ease of movement, swan shot should be removed from the leger until just enough remain to sink the bait, then by merely lifting the rod, the bait can be made to move to a different position.

Regrettably, a night-fishing ban is in force on many southern barbel waters and this prevents anglers from taking full advantage of the situation I have described for, with the coming of daylight, these fish return to deeper water where they cease to feed.

Only during a period of cool, unsettled weather can these barbel be caught with any regularity during the day, and that is when float fishing comes into its own.

The most productive swims are the deep runs between weed beds. Such swims are fished most effectively if the float is set at a depth some 3ft or 4ft greater than that of the water and held back a little, allowing the hook bait of maggots to search the irregularities of the river bed. A continual stream of loose maggots should be fed through the swim, and if this is kept up barbel will feed periodically throughout the day. Occasionally, a larger barbel may be hooked, so I never use a line weaker than 4lb for this style of fishing.

However enjoyable this sport may be, there are other advantages to be gained from the visits paid to these fast, gravelly rivers.

Much can be learned from the capture of small barbel and I treat the first few weeks of each new season as a time to experiment with different baits and new techniques–a task to which I give time only grudgingly later in the season.

As August draws to a close, even these small barbel become dour and difficult to catch. The fun is over and the more serious quest for specimens is about to begin.

Autumn is the season when heavyweights put in an appearance, but first, an increased flow of highly oxygenated water is required. An autumnal flood is usually a very short-lived affair, but while it lasts, barbel become so satiated that when the river returns to its normal height they stop feeding for a time. Nevertheless, it is as if the extra oxygenation of the water has triggered off some feeding mechanism for, even if there are no more floods, barbel will continue to feed periodically until the first hard frosts appear in November.

Periods when barbel restart feeding appear to be activated by changes in the weather and, because they feed for such a short time, one has to be both dedicated and something of an opportunist to take advantage of them.

At this time of the year I keep a careful eye on the weather and organise the less important side of my life in a way which allows me to make haste to the river as soon as possible after hearing a favourable weather forecast.

These visits entail a sixty-mile drive, often with time for only an hour or two's fishing at the other end. And even when I spend all day at the river, these big fish are unlikely to be caught except during a short period at dawn and again at dusk. It follows, then, that perfection in tackle and technique is desirable if full advantage is to be taken of the seemingly rare occasions when big barbel feed.

My biggest phobia is concerned with the unreliability of nylon monofilament. This dates back to an evening when a 7lb b.s. line, purchased only a month previously, snapped like cotton as increased pressure slowed down what was to be the final run of a barbel estimated as weighing more than 13lb.

Since then, I have never kept a line more than a few weeks before discarding it, and each time I fish I break off yards of line before I am satisfied with its strength.

One of the most effective barbel baits is a large piece of beef sausage meat, and I try to ensure that I always have a fresh supply. I have found that if these fish are at all hungry this bait will be taken soon after it settles on the bottom, and so only rarely do I allow my baited hook to remain in one place for longer than fifteen minutes.

Light legering is the most effective way of searching a swim and is far more exciting than watching a float. My method of detecting bites is to rest the line across the finger tips of my left hand. This method is extremely sensitive, and the uncanny sensation of being in contact with a feeding barbel can be an almost unnerving experience if very large fish are known to be in the swim.

The type of bite felt by the angler is determined by the factors which initiated the sudden burst of feeding activity. If the river is high and coloured, bites will be quite violent and often without warning. Similar bites are experienced as a thunderstorm moves away, but these apart, barbel feed in a more inhibited way when the river is at its normal height.

A few days of Indian summer will be enough to set off the feeding mechanism once more, but only for a brief period at dawn and again at dusk. During

Fishing the Thames at Hampton Court Long Water—always a favourite weekend spot.

such spells a delicate positioning of the bait is essential, for a barbel will move the bait only a few inches before rejecting it. All that will be felt is a momentary and almost imperceptible increase in pressure on the line which, for all its subtlety, will mean only one thing to the experienced angler – a barbel and a big one at that!

Concentration becomes a problem when bites are few and far between. A lapse can lead to missed bites, as will the seemingly helpless immobility which is the result of trying too hard.

The best thing to do is to relax, but this is not easy when the stakes are so high. I can best illustrate this problem by describing a fishing session that took place in October a few years ago.

For weeks the river had been low and the weather cool, with a dry easterly wind. There had been no sign of barbel when, towards the end of the month, the weather changed and a gale blew up from the south-west. All night long it raged and for most of the following day it blew hard until, about four in the afternoon, the air was once more still and considerably warmer.

With eager hands I assembled my tackle and crept to the water's edge, fully expecting a bite from my very first cast, but although I searched the swim, an hour passed uneventfully. Then, without warning, pressure was increased on the line and, just as quickly, it had gone.

Instead of striking, I had sat there immobile and, hardly believing that I had failed to react to the first barbel bite for weeks, I recast and the same process was repeated. One can only leave the reader to imagine just how helpless one feels in such circumstances.

There was only one thing to do – stop fishing for a while. I poured myself some coffee and sat back to contemplate my lack of skill.

A few minutes later, feeling a little calmer, I cast for a third time and waited, hoping against hope that my last chance had not gone. This time fortune smiled on me, and as the line tightened I struck and found myself playing an 11lb barbel.

A barbel angler soon learns to count his blessings and when, a few days later, icy margins heralded the end of another season's barbel fishing, I felt more than a little grateful that the path to success is not always as smooth as one would sometimes wish.

This, then, is my approach to barbel fishing. An approach in which the pattern of my addiction, aroused by the first sightings of these fish in late spring, gradually intensifies until, during the mellow days of autumn, I can think of nothing else but the quest for these mysterious and unpredictable fish.

In all this time barbel have been synonymous with the weather, so it is hardly surprising that the coming of winter effects a cure, a process which, contrary to its growth, takes place almost overnight. The pressure is off and I breathe a sigh of relief when I realise that I am free once more to enjoy the pleasure afforded by less demanding species. Yet I know that, within a few short months, the old feelings will be rekindled and the now familiar pattern repeated.

When the weather is good and the fish are biting, there are few more pleasant Thames haunts than this stretch of the river near Chertsey.

25

HOOKED

THE DAY the Ramsey family accepted a friend's invitation to try angling, it wasn't the fish that got hooked. It was the Ramsey family – and there are ten of them old enough to cast a line.

The Ramseys are pictured here, preparing for another full day's fishing. There's Mum, Mrs Dorothy Ramsey, 37, holding young Simon; Dad, Mr Tony Ramsey, 40; Patricia, 17, Paul, 15, Carol, 14, Christopher, 13, Richard, 9, Andrew, 8, and Susan, 7. The tenth angler, twelve-year-old Stephen, was in hospital when the photograph was taken.

The Ramseys' craze for fishing started six years ago. Now they've all got their own rods, licences, keepnets, bait tins and stools. They never miss a chance to use them. Every weekend they pile into their van for excursions to rivers, lakes and canals.

Last summer, Mrs Ramsey took the family for a fishing holiday – for six weeks! Dad, a floor-layer, joined them at weekends after work. Said Mrs Ramsey at their home in Winrose Approach, Leeds: 'We haven't forced the kids to join in. They are mad keen.'

The Ramseys fish mainly for perch, bream and roach – and occasionally trout. Family record-holder is Carol, who once landed a 3lb pike.

Are you all sitting comfortably? Then we'll begin...

Up North, they say, the anglers are hardier and they don't mind where they perch so long as the sport is good. We would not wish to get involved in the debate, but this young Yorkshire competitor was certainly prepared for hours of cold discomfort during the annual Worsall-to-Yarm contest.

BILLY LANE SAYS..

BILLY LANE is Britain's most famous match angler—and her only World Champion. He has won countless awards since he began his match-fishing career as a small boy. Billy and his family run a fishing tackle shop in Coventry, and spend most of their spare time fishing in competitions or answering the queries that pour into their shop every week.

Match anglers are the trend setters

AT no time have the techniques of angling developed at greater speed than they have in the last decade . . . and in the case of freshwater fishing for coarse fish, most of the major discoveries have surely stemmed from the match anglers.

Spurred on by the natural appeal of competition – to say nothing of the bigger financial returns that can be won – matchmen have done, and are still doing, more to forward our angling than any single group.

I am not saying this because I'm a matchman myself. It's simply that I was asked by the editor what I thought was the most important aspect of our branch of the sport, and there's no doubt in my mind that this is it.

Match fishing, I'd go so far as to say, is now the anvil on which most of the top ideas are being forged today. Furthermore, the crop of anglers who are busy doing the forging are of a general standard which would have been undreamed of before the war. There are so many good 'uns, with so many good ideas.

The proof of all this? Consider the fantastic improvements there have been in the last ten years in legering techniques, and then ask yourselves who dreamed up most of them.

Think of all the fascinating and *efficient* bite indicators that have been invented by match fishing's leger men, particularly the swing tip; in certain parts of the country, this is now considered the *only* technique worth employing.

But there has also been a revolution in float fishing, again sparked by the match-fishing fraternity. In my own case, there was the family of sliding floats I invented for fishing deeper water. Today, they are in universal use. Take just two more of the 'impact' floats of today – the zoomer, for fishing far off with little resistance, and the 'stick', accepted by some as the Rolls-Royce of trotting floats. Both were produced by the matchmen.

I could go on, but I hope I have already demonstrated that match fishing is more to angling than a bunch of blokes hell bent on pot-hunting. We've been accused of going mad with bait, for instance. But it has always been by chaps who have probably been making use of our ideas in other directions but who, publicly, don't want to give us credit for anything.

For me, life would not be the same without match fishing. Most of our breed, I have found, are a wonderful bunch of fellows whose sense of fair play, with very few exceptions, is the greatest. And I like the discipline of the game.

He goes to that draw bag, gets to his swim, and his job is to catch as many fish from it as he can. No matter if he doesn't win the match. That is not nearly so important to a matchman as most people would like to believe.

His main concern is to beat the two lads on either side of him. If he has done that, he has done all he can. If it also means he has won the match, that is an added bonus which will no doubt make him extremely happy.

What starts a man on the match-fishing trail? In my experience, few anglers take up fishing as match-

Everything at the ready, for speed is the essence of match fishing, as champion Billy Lane points out.

men from the outset. In fact, I believe that the majority of those who eventually become match anglers have been frustrated in their early days by the quality of the waters they have been able to fish, although there are some who just drift into match fishing as a logical development from their normal fishing.

Nevertheless, the men who do best are almost invariably those who come from the most deprived areas in the angling sense . . . men whose first fishing years were a constant battle, generally in industrial areas, to scrape together a few puny fish from water which will only just sustain life.

Add the spirit of competition, however, to what could otherwise be rather glum occasions, and you have the reason why match fishing captures the imaginations of so many. Eventually, they want to fish this way all the time.

Mind you, it's no good going in for matching unless you are really keen. If you are considering the change, there are two things you must do.

First, you must decide to give up all other branches of angling at the outset. There is no reason why you should not return to them later for a bit of variety.

Second, you must be convinced that you are good enough to succeed. The more strongly you hold this opinion, the better and the faster will be your progress.

The best time to begin? Ideally, when you are a youngster. You can't start too soon, for this way your technique develops easily and naturally, and your power to absorb new ideas is at its sharpest.

Another question I am often asked: What is the matchman's greatest asset? Without doubt, I say it is the ability to use one's tackle like some smooth-running machine. Every movement should be sure, swift and simple and made almost unconsciously.

I can tell at a glance whether a man has this asset, whatever his fishing experience. Such a man exudes efficiency and is a pleasure to watch.

I had a practical example of this during a recent appearance at the National Angling Show in London. I was demonstrating at the casting pool with a centre pin reel, and I was constantly being told by spectators how impressed they had been by the apparent ease with which I handled an item of tackle many find somewhat difficult. I found it hard to accept their praise, for I had been doing something I didn't even have to think about; yet when I stirred my memory, I realised that I had done quite a lot of practice many years before.

In my own case, most of it had been done under the watchful eyes of an angling father who was more than keen that I should succeed. Failure to do the right thing often resulted in a thick ear!

Practice is, of course, an extremely good thing. Believe me, all those tales about anglers practising accuracy with groundbait by hurling lumps of the stuff into buckets placed at a strategic distance away from them really are true. Some of you may laugh at such antics. But for me, they are all part of the truth about what makes a match fisherman great.

The reason for all this efficiency should be obvious. It's a question of time. By being as fast as you can, you will have your bait in the water much longer than the next man's . . . a logical enough reason if ever there was one.

Just how efficient should you get? Well, here is my favourite test. FISH BLINDFOLD. By this I mean you should go with a friend to a water you know well, and cast and groundbait with your eyes covered. If you achieve accuracy in these circumstances, your angling instincts are coming along fine.

In the early days, it is always best to restrict your match fishing to one particular kind of water, and to master it completely before moving to pastures new. Some are better starters than others.

A man who, for instance, begins his match fishing life on a canal is likely to progress faster; from the outset, he must learn to develop a subtle approach, because fish in this setting really have to be tempted

TRADE MARK OF A CHAMP

A picture to make any match angler's heart beat a little faster. Here is Billy Lane, a net bulging with fish, as he prepares for the weigh-in. Some champion!

on to the hook. If, on the other hand, he begins in a river like the Trent, he won't have such an advantage; here the fish feed decisively, and mostly it is a question of their being 'on' or not.

Canal fish have a chance to inspect your bait, whereas in a river they have to grab it while they can or they've had it.

Money is a bogyman often brought up in the name of match anglers. It is, of course, a factor, for there can be a lot of it floating about on some fixtures. But it is not nearly so important as many of our detractors would have it.

There are literally thousands of matchmen who fish every week for nothing more than a few bob and are perfectly content.

Obviously, most of them like to win some money, but the price of trying can vary a great deal and this is another question the budding matchman must ask himself. How much can I afford?

On a small water in a little club match, the outlay would not be large, but a big Open event could run a man into a bill of £5 or more. All I say is that if you suit your match fishing to your pocket, then you should find contentment.

Now if all this has seemed something of a defence of match fishing I make no apology, for at this particular time we seem constantly under fire from critics who say we take up too much water, we overfish too much water, we're money mad or we're just tiddler-snatchers.

All I ask is that these same critics should stop and ask themselves just how much match fishing has given to angling, compared with what it has taken. And it must leave us in credit.

An appreciative audience gathers as the catch is weighed on the bank of the Great Ouse Relief Channel at King's Lynn, a well-known spot for match-men. Nothing, of course, to compare with the Match of the Century, pictured below.

WHO CAN IT BE?

A MOST UNLIKELY situation for a most unlikely angler—and our odds if we were in the betting business would be something in the region of a million to one against your guessing the identity of the well-disguised figure in this picture. The scene is the Bridge-water Canal at Sale, Cheshire, and the mystery figure is a world champ. No, not Billy Lane! A slightly daintier figure, who happened to be in Manchester on business and decided to snatch an hour off to try her luck in the canal. Her name? Miss Reita Faria, who was rather better known as Miss World than as an angler. Well, it makes a nice picture, and after all, Miss Faria is no stranger to angling. 'Back home in India I can usually guarantee to catch something,' she said.

A FISHING ROD IS PART OF MY LUGGAGE

Colin Willock is one of the best-known names in angling journalism. He is author of several books and writes for the 'Sun', 'Observer', 'Angler's Mail' and 'Shooting Times'. He is head of Anglia TV's Natural History Unit and writes their 'Survival' series.

says

Colin

Willock

THE inconsistencies of the human sporting mind are fascinating, even, or perhaps particularly, to the owner of one of these imperfect pieces of mechanism. How else shall I explain that fishing and shooting are equal passions with me?

Shooting appeals to me only within my native boundaries. I am a dedicated wildfowler. Show me a winter estuary in Britain and I am not satisfied until I am knee-deep in its muddy creeks, waiting for the widgeon to flight.

Take me to a lake in the Rift Valley of Africa, where duck abound in millions, and I do not want to take my gun out of its case. In fact, I could not do so anyway, since I never have a gun with me.

Fishing, for some reason I am at a loss to explain, is totally different. I am willing and anxious to fish anywhere. I regard a fishing rod as being as much a part of my luggage as the labels on my suitcase. In fact, more so.

I can get by without a spare shirt and shoes. I honestly do not think I could bear to travel without knowing that I had at least some basic fishing gear with me.

I've fished in some pretty odd places and I hope to fish in some a good deal odder before I've done. I suppose the most exciting water I've ever wet a line in was the Nile, very close to its source in Uganda.

I was making a film for the TV natural history series, 'Survival'. Believe it or not, we had been catching far bigger quarry than fish on the end of our lines. We had been chasing three-ton white rhinos in a truck and lassooing them in order to shift them away from poachers and into the safety of Murchison Falls National Park.

Now that the job was done, we had a few days to spend in the Park while our catches settled down to their new home. This was the time to get out the fishing rods.

I had brought a fly rod (for tiger fish of all

Thames lover

Mr John Fraser, Labour M.P. for Norwood, decided to try his luck after a fifteen-inch carp had been found by workmen near the House of Commons. But his luck was out. So, too, was that of five teams who fished for five hours from barges in mid-stream on the Thames, a competition inspired by Mr Desmond Plummer, leader of the Greater London Council. Meanwhile, the fight for a cleaner Thames goes on.

things!), a salmon spinning rod and a fixed spool reel loaded with 8lb line. This was far heavier than I normally use back home, but something told me that any fish I met up with in Africa was likely to be that much bigger and fiercer.

The warden of Murchison Falls Park, Roger Wheater, took one look at this rig and said kindly that he thought it might be a little light for what we had in mind.

In the mile of whirlpools below the Falls lived some truly gigantic Nile perch. The record for this species is somewhere way over the 300lb mark. The record for the Park was only just over half that. Even so, a 160lb Nile perch is not to be sneered at.

We set off under the burning sun in the Park's powerful anti-croc-poaching boat. That the poachers had not been entirely successful was evident along the seven-mile ride upriver to the Falls. Crocs of up to 12 feet long slid into the water as we roared by.

Sometimes we caught unawares one that had ventured fifty yards back from the water. When the sound of the motor disturbed him, he jacked himself up into a leg-extended position and ran at an astounding pace back to the water's edge.

I learned from Roger Wheater that these big crocs were our direct competitors. They constantly 'fished' for big Nile perch, too. They caught 100lb fish crossways in their snouts, just as a pike might seize a roach, shook it until it was dead and then turned it and swallowed it.

I only hoped they had left some big perch for us. Apparently, to an adult croc, a 100lb perch is just a light snack.

Murchison Falls itself is one of the wonders of Africa. The Nile, a powerful river about the size of the Thames at Henley, roars down a series of falls and cataracts for about thirty miles as it comes out of Lake Kyoga below Lake Victoria. Then, at Murchison, it meets a great barrier of super-hard rock. It has spent thousands of years cutting the softer rock away until it has come up against this apparently immovable object.

Nevertheless, it has done its best to break through. The result of thousands of years of hard work is a narrow slit in the cliff face, just over twenty feet wide. The entire river hurls itself at this narrow chasm and explodes in its effort to force itself through.

Below this explosion, in the whirlpools for a mile downstream in the gorge, live the biggest of the Nile perch. This is where I aimed to spin for them with 8lb line!

But we were by no means in the swim yet. First we had to make a mile-long foot safari along the banks of the gorge. Anyone accustomed to well-trimmed towpaths had better think again before he goes perch fishing in the Nile. There is no accepted track. All the way we were forcing our way through tall ferns that grow in the moist air from the river and the whirlpools' spray.

At any moment you are likely to find an elephant blocking your path. Elephants do not understand that fishermen are impatient people. You cannot show them your permit and ask them politely to move out of your swim. If you do so, they are quite likely to take your head off. You have no alternative, therefore, but to stand stock-still at a respectful distance and hope that they will decide to go away. This can quite easily take all day.

On this occasion we did not meet an elephant, though subsequently I have made exactly this time-consuming encounter on this very track. Today we met a spitting cobra.

Spitting cobras are remarkably accurate. They spit at anything bright they can spot on their adversary's person. The target, therefore, is invariably the eyes. If their venom scores a bull's-eye, it can cause at least temporary blindness. They are accurate at ranges of more than six feet.

The spitting cobra that appeared from under a rock and spat at Roger Wheater, who was leading our column, was fortunately only a tiddler. His venom arched out and fell short.

I was quite happy to leave things that way, at, say, fifteen-all, but Roger wanted that small snake alive for the Park museum. So he dived into the rocks, where it occurred to me bigger and better cobras might be lurking, and grabbed the offender smartly behind the head so that it couldn't unload the rest of its venom through its fangs.

Then he asked if anyone had a container in which

to carry the little beast. Unfortunately I had a plastic holder for the telephoto lens to my camera. Since this was already perforated at one end, in went the cobra to share my haversack with my fishing tackle.

The wildlife delights of that day were by no means over. Murchison gorge, it appeared, was inhabited by every tsetse fly squadron in East Africa. We were all they had been waiting for.

If you have ever been plagued by mosquitoes at evening rise, believe me you have not really suffered. If you have been eaten alive by ants while sitting in a tench swim, you have not even touched the fringe of the insect world's beastliness.

The tsetses came in with a low-level attack, firing what seemed to be barbed rockets. Their stings went straight through my remarkably thick skin, which has been known to blunt hypodermic needles, and raised a series of bumps that made my skin feel like a cucumber.

Hopping with pain and swatting like maniacs, we began to spin for those legendary perch. Roger used a six-inch Pfleuger plug armed with three fearsome trebles. He fished with a rod that would have held a small sea shark and a sea Mitchell fitted with 14lb breaking line, and he was soon into a fish.

In that fierce water, the Nile perch gives a remarkable account of itself. The turbulence below the Falls is terrific. So is the noise of the falling water. Much of the time we were delightfully drenched with cool, needle-fine spray.

The Nile perch proved to be a deep, jagging fighter, rather like its distant British relative. In this water, even a 30lb tiddler (only live-bait size) gave a fight to remember.

Catching 'em young!

Lucky are the young people of Matching Green, in Essex. Reserved for them is the fishing in the village pond. The children share a keepnet, and when the day is done they count the number of roach, carp and rudd they have caught . . . then return them to the pond. Lucky are the fish of Matching Green.

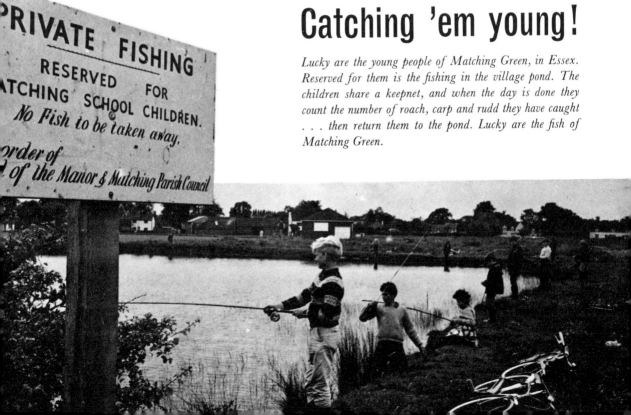

With 8lb line and plug scaled down to match, I had my work cut out. My smaller plug, about three inches long, caught fish to match Roger's in size and fighting quality, but I had them on twice as long, since it was impossible to 'horse' them in that kind of current.

All the time we fished – and between us we caught thirty perch up to 60lb. Nothing really to get excited about, but the fish eagles circled overhead giving that tingling, whistling cry that is often called the sound of Africa. Possibly they were jealous that we were catching fish and they weren't.

In the end, I didn't catch the biggest fish. That fell to Roger Wheater. But I was quite happy with a brace of forty-pounders when they came out of that extraordinary, frightening whirlpool, fins bristling and clear eyes winking with an evil yellow light. They seemed just the sort of creature one should be catching in such a dramatic setting.

As I landed my first forty-pounder, the fish we had caught earlier were already spitted on green sticks and sizzling deliciously over the flames of a fire lit by our African game scouts.

A couple of fair catches, you might sa

Fly fishing will tempt the ladies, where maggots will make them shudder! Here a Scottish angler nets a 4½lb grilse; right, a fine trout from the Costa Beck, a Yorkshire chalk stream.

BIG GAME FISHING

JOHN GODDARD, an all-round angler, is managing director of Efgeeco, the tackle makers. He is an expert fly fisherman and a noted authority on trout flies, but in winter he turns to sea fishing and deepsea adventure. Here he poses (left) with an Atlantic big-eyed tunny of 245lb, the largest ever caught off Madeira.

by John Goddard

THE gentle hum from the twin diesels of the big game launch *Albacora* was suddenly shattered by a shout of 'Fish on!'—and the scream of a reel check. We were trolling for tunny in the tranquil, blue waters off the island of Madeira and this was the first fish to take one of the three lures we were trolling.

As the boat slowed down, 'Polly' Policansky had already settled into the fighting chair, tightened the brake on his 12/0 reel and struck the fish with all his strength to set the hook. The fish, which we were now fairly sure was a tunny, was ripping line off the reel at an incredible rate, and it seemed to us that its one ambition in life, at that moment, was to reach the bed of the ocean over a thousand fathoms below us as quickly as possible.

The first run of this powerful fish took off nearly 300 yards of line, and by this time the reel was so hot that 'Polly' was yelling for us to cool it with water. Eventually, its first run was stopped and with this length of line out, 'Polly' sensibly slackened off the star drag.

He then began work seriously on the tunny with a fast, but steady, pumping action. But the fish was still far too fresh to appreciate this treatment, and with a lunge that slammed the angler against his harness and nearly brought him up out of the chair, the tunny commenced another hard run which took out a further 100 yards of line.

'Polly' now started steadily pumping the fish again, and slowly gained line. Every now and then the fish gave a savage jerk of its head which almost tore the rod out of the angler's hand.

After an hour's hard work, the tunny was showing definite signs of weakening; most of the line had been recovered and we were all peering intently over the side of the boat for the first sign of the fish. Suddenly, the skipper of the boat shouted 'There it is,' and in the very clear water we could all see its outline about 100 feet down, directly below the boat.

Up to now the skipper at the wheel had found little to do, as the fish had fought it out in the deep water more or less below the boat. Now, as the double leader came in sight, handling of the launch was of prime importance. One miscalculation on his part, in letting the adversary get immediately below the keel, and the 'screws' would have cut through the line in a flash.

At long last, the double leader came in over the top roller of the rod and the great, silvery fish rolled on the surface about twenty yards from the boat. The tunny was still fairly fresh, and it sounded on at least half-a-dozen occasions before the wire leader finally came within Leslie Moncrieff's reach.

Directly Leslie had a firm grip on the wire leader, I shouted to 'Polly' to release his brake and then handed Leslie our large break-head gaff. Within seconds the gaff dug in, and the first tunny hooked on this holiday was ours.

Weighed after we returned to port, it went a little over 185lb and had taken about one hour and twenty minutes to subdue. No monster, of course,

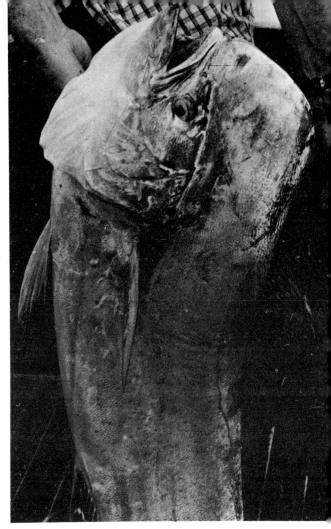

The ugly-mug of the big game world! A close-up of the very blunt head of a bull dolphin, caught off Madeira.

but a good size for this particular species of tunny.

I was one of a small party of anglers testing out the fishing in the waters around Madeira. In the last three or four years I have been trying the fishing in various areas around the European and Mediterranean coasts in an effort to locate good big game fishing.

I had decided to try Madeira for this trip after studying charts of the ocean surrounding the Island. Prospects looked good, although as far as I could gather, little fishing had been done in this area and no reliable information was available. The second member of our party was Leslie Moncrieff, one of the top British anglers in this branch of our sport, and to make up our complement I had also invited Hymie Policansky, a South African, who has had a wealth of big game fishing experience over the years in the waters around the Cape.

We flew from London to Madeira, via Lisbon, and I shall never forget my first sight of the Island as we came in to land on the airstrip, which had been literally hacked out of the side of the mountain. It was late afternoon and the setting sun was sparkling on the blue waters of the bay as the plane banked.

The awe-inspiring, sheer cliffs were throwing deep shadows over the lazy surf as it broke on the rocks at sea level. From the tops of these cliffs the land rose in steep terraces, covered in verdant green vegetation and dotted with little white, red-roofed cottages up to the misty heights of the high mountains in the centre of the Island.

Apart from the scenic splendour of these mountains, we were later to realise that they were a valuable asset to our fishing. Due to their height and the fact that the prevailing winds in this latitude blow continuously from the North-East throughout most of the summer from May to September, the South side of the Island, including the capital Funchal, where we were based, enjoys exceptionally calm seas.

During our fourteen days' stay, we did not have one day in which we could not put to sea, and I am sure most deep sea fishermen will appreciate the importance of this. The temperature during the summer averaged 75 degrees, which is ideal for both the fishing and holiday enjoyment.

Our biggest problem when fishing abroad has always been the location of suitable boats, but in Funchal we were well catered for in this respect, as the local Tourist Board has a fully-equipped, twin-screw, big game launch available with crew, and there are also several well-equipped local craft available.

The tunny fishing we found quite fabulous, but more of that later. The first week we concentrated on smaller species of game fish and inshore fishing. Barracuda are to be caught for most of the year, and are most commonly encountered along the rocky

coastline around the eastern end of the Island. Also, the bluefish or anchova are found in the same locality.

A little farther out to sea, bonito are to be found in large shoals and although the commercial fishermen catch these in vast quantities, we were unable to do so. This, of course, was not surprising, as these fish are notoriously difficult to catch until the right lure or method is discovered.

Three miles or more from the shore in the open ocean are to be found the occasional wahoo, and dolphin or dorado are quite common. In fact, we caught quite a lot of these, and give them top marks among the smaller species of game fish. Most of the dorado we caught varied between 10lb and 20lb, but we also caught several between 30lb and 40lb and the largest taken by Leslie during our visit was a magnificent bull dolphin of 44lb.

I shall never forget the first of these larger fish that we caught. At the time we were trolling for tuna with small feathered lures and with our medium outfits, which was rather a pity as these fish should be taken on light outfits for maximum sport. The dolphin took Leslie's small red-and-white feather with a smashing strike, and as soon as it felt the hook bite home, it cleared the water in one stupendous leap.

These fish are so fast that by the time Leslie had adjusted the star drag, the dolphin had covered at least 150 yards and its next breathtaking leap was well out to the side of the boat. During the next five minutes it completely cleared the water at least four times, and treated us to three spectacular sizzling runs which peeled line off the reel at an

The big game launch Albacora, *with Ponta de Sao Lourenco, Madeira, in the background.*

42

alarming rate.

This dolphin fought on the surface most of the time, which is, of course, typical of the species, and due to its speed and bewildering changes of direction, Leslie was really hard pressed to keep a tight line on it.

After ten minutes' hard work, Leslie was streaming with perspiration, but the fish was beginning to tire. As I wanted to get a good colour picture of one of these dolphins when it first surfaced near the launch, I climbed on to the top of the flying bridge with the camera ready. I saw the line cutting up through the water, and the next second the dolphin was rolling on the surface.

I am afraid the photograph was never taken, as I was completely spellbound by the dazzling display of colours on the fish and by the time I had gathered my wits, the gaff had bitten in and the opportunity had passed.

As a result of our fourteen days' holiday, we are now convinced that the big future for fishing in this area lies with the tunny fishing, and as a direct result of our visit and the success that we attained, we understand that the Madeiran Tourist Board are considering providing a fully-equipped sports fishing centre.

The potential of the tunny fishing can be judged by the fact that we concentrated on them for only the last three days of our holiday; furthermore September, the month we were there, is considered a poor month. During the period we were in Madeira, the fifty commercial tunny boats working from the Island took fewer than sixty fish. Despite this, we caught several tunny all on trolled feathers and the best tipped the scales at 245lb. We also had another good fish of 238lb.

All the tunny we caught were the species called the Atlantic Big Eye, and when one considers that the world record for this species is only 295lb it will be realised that there is a strong possibility of a new world record from this area.

During the height of the tunny season, which is from March to May, the catch by the commercial boats is about 700 to 800 fish per day. Another interesting fact is that the giant bluefin tunny are also present during this period and on most days,

Leslie Moncrieff proudly displays a magnificent bull dolphin of 44lb, which set up a new record in Madeira for this species.

two or three of these gigantic fish are brought into the market.

Finally, and really to whet the appetite of the big game fisherman, marlin are regularly seen, and every day that we visited the fish market, small broadbill swordfish were in evidence.

For the average British angler, big game fishing as recounted above may not be possible, as apart from the considerable expense involved for the daily hire of a suitable boat and special tackle, there is

A good day's catch after an adventurous day aboard the Albacora. *Left to right are Leslie Moncrieff, Hymie Policansky and John Goddard, standing by their mixed bag of dorado and tunny.*

also the expense of fares to reach this rather distant location. However, it is quite possible that travel agents may soon be able to offer package deal holidays specially for anglers to such locations at greatly reduced rates.

In the meantime, I am happy to say there are numerous other centres nearer home where the keen sea angler can enjoy excellent deep sea fishing combined with a family holiday, and although this type of fishing may not be quite so glamorous as big game fishing, the distinction between the two is very slight.

To mention briefly just a few of these locations I would start with Gibraltar, as during the last few years the Rock has established quite a reputation for deep sea fishing. The air fare is very reasonable considering the distance involved, accommodation is good, and the fishing at times can be very exciting.

It should also be mentioned that the social side is *par excellence*, particularly during the regular angling festivals that are held during the season.

There are plenty of good boats available, tackle if required, and the main species of fish are blue sharks, pargo and grouper. The latter are a very large member of the bream family and average thirty or forty pounds in weight. In the very deep water off the Rock, they can be quite a handful on rod and line.

Another very good centre in this vicinity is Sagres, a small, undeveloped fishing village on the Southern tip of Portugal. There is first-class accommodation available here at the Government-run Pousada, which is also very inexpensive, or there is a five-star hotel, The Baleria. This is a very sparsely inhabited area of Portugal and is completely unspoilt, and for the family there are numerous secluded beaches with miles of golden sands, within walking distance of the village.

The best month for the fishing is undoubtedly October, and at this time of the year migratory surface game fish such as bonito, albacore and the famed bluefish are to be caught. These are mainly caught by trolling offshore, but apart from these fish there is also the possibility, while drift fishing deep baits, of hooking large mako, porbeagle or hammerhead sharks, or even the lordly broadbill swordfish.

The inshore or beach fishing for bass or mullet can also be very good, and there are also plenty of very large conger eels in the area. On several occasions I have seen congers of tremendous size brought in by the local commercial fishermen, some of them certainly in excess of 100lb.

Apart from the Southern coast of Portugal, the whole of the western seaboard offers excellent sport for a great variety of species. There are many very good bass beaches, and during September and October there is often a heavy run of tuna right along this coast.

A little south of Lisbon lies the picturesque fishing port of Sesimbra, a world-famous centre for the mighty broadbill swordfish, which every October attracts the stars of the big game fishing world, who pit their wits against this doughty adversary. The Hotel Espadarte is the nerve centre of this operation, as they handle all the boat bookings and other details, but it must be pointed out that this is a very expensive type of fishing. A mere corner on one of the specialised swordfish boats can cost at least £15 per day.

The Northern coast of Spain bordering on the Bay of Biscay is also another good area, and although I have not had personal experience of the actual fishing, I am sure it has considerable potential.

In a completely different direction and climate, the coast of Norway offers excellent deep sea fishing for very large cod, ling and pollack, etc., and a centre particularly worthy of mention on this coast is the Godoysund Hotel in Hardanger Fjord, which is a few miles north of Bergen.

This is a splendid new hotel situated on its own island in the fjord, in a setting of breathtaking beauty. The hotel, which specialises in all water sports, has its own fleet of small fishing boats available for guests, and within minutes of departing from the hotel excellent fishing for cod, pollack and even sea trout is available.

Finally, the Canary Islands, although a little farther afield, are particularly worthy of mention. Since these are situated off the north-west coast of Africa, they may appear far removed for the fisherman, but this is not so. There are many travel companies running charter flights to these islands at a very reasonable cost.

These islands offer considerable potential for the big game fisherman, as they are in an area that abounds with pelagic surface-feeding fish at certain periods of the year. To mention just a few, there are tunny, bluefish, albacore, bonito, barracuda, dolphin (dorado), wahoo and occasional marlin.

Unfortunately, little is known regarding sport fishing for these species of fish in this area, and consequently it is not possible to give the best months to fish for each species. However, there appears to be a resident population of large sharks of various species, and the blue sharks in particular grow to an enormous size in this area.

Up to now I have been discussing various locations for deep sea or big game fishing abroad, but it should be pointed out that there are many excellent locations for deep sea fishing in these islands of ours. Unfortunately, with the demise of tunny fishing in the North Sea off Scarborough in the fifties, the only serious big game fishing that was being practised in this country came to an abrupt end. The only true game fish that is now caught off our shores is the mako shark, but as these are taken only very occasionally and seldom on purpose, this hardly constitutes serious consideration.

We have wonderful cod fishing during the winter months off the South-East coast from resorts such as Deal, Dover, Folkestone and Newhaven, and every year many specimens of 30lb and over are landed.

Farther along the coast in the West Country, we are fortunate to find during the summer months many excellent marks for pollack fishing. These are an interesting species to catch and are fine sport on light tackle, particularly those taken off the deep water marks of twenty fathoms or more, as these grow to a goodly size averaging 12-14lb.

Good pollack are also found in quantities off the West and South coasts of Ireland, and in this area a favourite method of taking them is on large feathered hooks jigged from a boat near the sea bed.

Another species of deep sea fish common in the pollack areas I have mentioned is the ling, and specimens of 20lb and over are regularly caught in these parts.

An area that has only recently come into favour for deep sea fishing is the Western coast of Scotland. It is as yet largely undeveloped, but is now producing many interesting fish of specimen size, including all the species mentioned above and, in addition, haddock and very large skate.

However, the skate can hardly be classified as a deep sea fish as very often some of the largest specimens, usually common skate, are caught in quite shallow water, particularly off the West coast of Ireland which is famous for these ungainly creatures.

Conger fishing is now very popular in this country, and every season specimens exceeding 50lb are regularly caught, many of them from deep-water wrecks off the Irish and West Country coasts. But in my opinion, the most exciting deep sea fish to be caught on rod and line from our shores is the halibut, although I have formed this opinion only from hearsay, as I have yet to boat one myself.

However, several of my close friends have landed one or more of these fish and they are all unanimous that they are the most powerful and difficult fish of all to conquer; even with the heaviest of big game tackle, it is quite impossible to stop their first run when hooked.

Every year, odd specimens of these huge flat fish are caught from various places in Scotland and Ireland, but undoubtedly the most favoured area

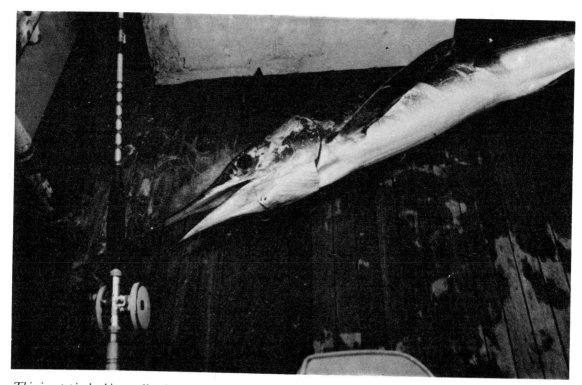

This is a typical white marlin photographed shortly after its capture. Note the comparatively small size of hook, which is hanging from the lower jaw.

for halibut at the moment is around the Orkney Islands off the North coast of Scotland. The largest halibut to be taken on rod and line off our coast is a fish of 161lb, recently captured from the Orkneys, but this record is likely to be short lived as the commercial long-liners in this vicinity regularly bring in fish of nearly double this weight.

In conclusion, this subject would hardly be complete without a short word about shark fishing in this country. Although this can hardly be termed big game fishing, it is the nearest approach we have, and during recent years it has quickly gained in popularity. The main quarry is the blue shark, which appear off our western coasts during the summer.

Shark fishing on a properly organised basis was first started shortly after World War II at Looe, Cornwall. Since then, other holiday resorts in this area and also off the North Cornish, Devon, South Wales and Irish coasts have become popular.

This form of fishing is usually practised well out to sea from a drifting boat. The heavy shark lines, usually baited with fresh mackerel, are fished at varying depths from five to more than twenty fathoms, and as the shark boat drifts with wind or tide, a trail of rubby dubby is laid to attract any sharks in the vicinity. The average size of the blue shark caught is around 60lb, but every year many in excess of 100lb are landed.

Initially this is a very exciting form of fishing; unfortunately, these small blues rarely put up much of a fight on the heavy tackle provided by most boats and one soon tires of this particular sport.

However, I would recommend every angler to give it a try. Occasionally a lucky angler will hook a large mako or porbeagle shark, and as these are often in excess of 200lb it is a battle to remember all his life–particularly if it be a mako, one of the most powerful and sporting of fish that an angler can hook on rod and line anywhere in the world.

Recently, one or two dedicated shark anglers have located a possible hot spot for these large mako and porbeagle off the eastern end of the Isle of Wight. During the 1968 season they had many successes with these fish, and towards the tail end of the season one of them, Trevor Prince, landed a

At the end of the day, a white marlin and several very handsome dorado.

huge porbeagle of 324lb which has now been submitted as a new British record.

Whether or not these particular species of sharks are regular visitors to this area remains to be seen. It is possible that their appearance may have been due to the exceptionally hot weather along this coast for the whole of the summer, resulting in higher water temperatures than usual.

SUCCESS

Percy Bolton, Hull tackle dealer, with a fine Arran haddock and dogfish caught off the Isle of Arran

●

. . . and this time Mr Bolton hauls aboard a fine codling from the same rich waters, in the picture below.

●

Over on the right, an all-action study as Michael Barrington-Martin safely boats a skate, to the obvious satisfaction of his colleague.

Alone I did it, says our fair lady—and a real smasher to be sure. Hunter and hunted alike!

IN SEARCH OF BIGGER TENCH

BY FRANK GUTTFIELD

FRANK GUTTFIELD is primarily a big fish man and known to most anglers as a tench specialist. To date he has caught three tench over 6lb and no fewer than eighty-two over 5lb. A well-known angling writer and author, he was founder of the old Arlesey Whopper Stoppers Group. Among his list of big fish are a fly-caught brown trout of 6lb 14oz, roach of 2lb 5oz, chub 5lb 12oz, and rudd 2lb 8oz. He wrote his first angling article at the age of sixteen.

I SUPPOSE it is only natural that most big-fish anglers have a passion for one particular species, and in my case there is no getting away from it—the tench is my favourite.

It seems an age since I set eyes upon my first tench, some nineteen years back when I was in short trousers. Those were the days I used to slither about the treacherous, wet clay banks of the Blue Lagoon and come home well and truly plastered.

These fish were not monsters, but little, light-coloured golden jobs of ¼lb to 1½lb. What is more important, they kept us happy; they sowed the seeds.

Four years later, one very wet day in July, I took my first look at a Bedfordshire lake that was to be my 'home' for many seasons. I stopped and peered through the bushes at two anglers who were just packing up in the 'bridge' swim. This was at the time of the greatest angling contest of them all, sponsored by the *Daily Mirror* and devised by Bernard Venables.

It was all happening. Bob Rutland and Brian (Titch) Collins heaved up two bulging keepnets of gleaming tench–tench far bigger than I'd ever seen, let alone caught. As I knelt and watched them being weighed, I was a darned sight more excited than their captors, though Brian (he was all of fifteen) looked just a little pleased when his best fish thumped the balance to the 5lb 7oz notch.

That was it. This was the foundation stone of my tench fishing career. I just couldn't wait to get one of those tench in MY net!

Soon I was at the pool, and I struck oil on my very first visit. That first fish scaled 4lb 14oz. It gave me a crazy fight and my Marvel fly rod nearly bent into a full circle.

My line was 9lb breaking strain, and the test curve of rod was about 7oz. Method quite simple, a float-fished lobworm—not exactly balanced tackle, was it?

I could have kissed that tench, and as I gazed at it, all I could think of was to catch more tench. The thought of bigger tench didn't really enter my mind. In fact, I thought I was jolly lucky to notch one as big as that on my maiden trip.

It was a great start, for despite what some of my more serious-minded friends think, I am positive that luck does play a part in angling and in the downfall of big fish.

Clicking on a new water first time IS lucky, and it can instil that important angling virtue, confidence. Luck can make or break a novice angler,

'On the bank and in the net—that's where I like to see 'em.' So says Frank Guttfield.

however keen he happens to be.

Years later, when I had considerable experience of the water, I took several new boys there under my wing, so to speak, and it was always the same. It took several days of hard slog before they got their first tench, and some gave up even before that. They were not so lucky; had they been, I'm sure it would have changed the pattern of their angling career.

As the years drifted by, my score of tench mounted. Three-pounders by the hundred, four-pounders by the score, with a handful of five-pounders each season. Little did I appreciate how fortunate I was to be situated within half an hour's cycle ride of this tench fishers' Mecca. Other splendid tench waters were even closer to my home, which was a good thing as I didn't know even one angler who owned a car in those days.

The seasons passed, and methods changed, swims changed, baits changed. First it was all close-in standard float stuff, then came the lift, long-range legering, the tube leger, freelining, cupping, the lot. Tactics changed, I changed. A new approach was called for.

For ten years I had been content to catch quantities of tench, building up quite a score of 'fives' in the process. Getting my name into the headlines of the angling papers with catches of *'A Dozen Four-Pounders Before Work'* was all very well, but now I wanted to catch BIGGER tench.

It must sound very smug, but I was getting rather bored with catching four- and even five-pound fish—and I wasn't yet holding the key of the door. I used to say to myself: 'If I keep catching those four- and five-pounders at this rate, that six-pounder is bound to come along.'

The closest I got was a beautiful brace of October fish of 5lb 12 oz and 5lb 14oz. If only they had taken my bait in June!

Every water has its limit, and at that time I reckon it must have been in the region of 6lb. Bigger fish were caught from time to time, but invariably they were spawners.

People tend to say to themselves: 'As there are so many five-pounders, there are bound to be a few six- or even seven-pounders in the water.'

A fine, slender 5lb 13oz October tench—very unlike the 'spawners' of June and July.

Unfortunately, there is no earthly reason why this should follow.

It's the same with carp. There are quite a few waters that yield numbers of 20lb fish, but never one of 30lb. This brings me back to the old maxim: *FIRST FIND YOUR FISH.*

As I didn't really know that the pool contained six-pounders, I decided I was flogging a dead horse and changed to Black Squirrels, another local lake where I KNEW such fish existed. Genuine six-pounders (non-spawners) had been caught there

and, what is more, I had seen fish that I estimated would scale 7lb. One fish, and only one, I reckoned could have been 8lb.

Other so-called experts, who only occasionally visited the water, made repeated claims of seeing tench 'well into double figures'. I watched that water almost daily for several seasons, and can only assume that they had viewed their fish through rose-tinted, polarised glasses.

Until somebody shows them to me, I just don't believe that double-figure tench exist. Doubting

Thomas, maybe, but I wish some of these fellows who see monsters everywhere they go would start producing the goods instead of theorising about them.

On this water I decided to discard the more conventional methods of baiting-up a swim etc., having tried them for a couple of seasons. More off-beat methods were tried, and all manner of baits and techniques were experimented with. I felt that these bigger-than-normal tench had to be hunted in a different way; they were not the sort of fish that would pop up in a big bag. They were loners and kept to the confines of the heavily weeded areas.

One of the trials, using a twitched lobworm on a swanshot leger, yielded my very first heart-throb, a beauty of 6lb 4oz without a trace of spawn. Two weeks later came a second big fish of 4oz larger. Again, this was a bit lucky, wasn't it? All those years, then two such fish in the short space of a fortnight.

Then came an interlude of two seasons in my tench fishing, and lo and behold!, in my first full season back at Black Squirrels, I had a third six-pounder. An ounce over the mark this time, but again a clean fish.

So where do we go from here? Seven-pounders, records? No I don't think so, as I just haven't found a water where fish of such proportions exist in sufficient numbers to merit an onslaught.

I did mention that I had seen seven-pounders in Black Squirrels, but I reckon there are only half a dozen in as many acres. The odds are too slim. If only someone would take me to one of those waters that teem with double-figure tench, my ambitions would be less modest.

But do you know what? Only the other day I heard that those tiddler tench we used to catch at the Blue Lagoon are now bigger. Very much BIGGER! So it looks as if next season will see me reliving those boyhood days.

An early season tench weighing 6lb 1oz, captured by Guttfield, and (below) an autumn tench netted from a pool in Hampshire.

RANDOM FISH TALES

RICHARD WILLS, Editor of *The World of Angling*, has been fishing since he was knee high to a tackle box. He has made thousands of new friends with his amusing and off-beat stories in his Friday column in the *Sun* newspaper. Here, specially selected for *The World of Angling*, are just a few of those stories . . .

ABOUT the limping man from the off-licence ...and a 'roach' with a past...

ABOUT John's tench and Christopher's carp and young Mr Lister the shark-catcher...

ABOUT the pike in the bath...and a mighty splash on the Biggleswade stretch...

ABOUT Scarface...

A WILY 18-year-old fish failed to spot the hook in a tiny piece of bread on the bottom of a Hertfordshire gravel pit late one evening last week–and started an angling investigation that is likely to ripple through the sport for years. The elderly fish weighed 3lb 11oz 2dr, and in the light of a torch on the banks of Northmet Lake, Cheshunt, it looked every inch a roach.

That made it a very spectacular catch indeed for angler Richard Whitehall, of Clapton, East London, who knew that only two bigger roach have been recorded by the British Record Fish Committee.

But by Monday this week, Mr Whitehall's moment of glory had turned to bitter disappointment. His fish turned out to be the hybrid result of an affair in the dim, watery past between a great-great-grandfather roach and a bream.

Most hybrids are dreaded by big-fish hunters, who must seek only pure species to secure a niche in angling history, and roach are becoming their biggest headache in this respect.

Mr Whitehall's 'roach' was the biggest teaser for years, and it took the combined sleuthing of Mr Whitehall, who is an experienced taxidermist, the weekly fishing newspaper *Angler's Mail* and scientists at the Natural History Museum to unravel the mystery. Everything checked out satisfactorily— including the vital pharyngeal (throat) teeth—in comparison with the Museum's collection of roach specimens.

Then the scientists called for blow-ups of the newspaper's photographs of the fish—which revealed that Mr Whitehall's fish had a few more scales along its lateral line than is allowed in the best roach circles—and there were four rays too many in one fin.

This unusually thorough investigation of a fish, whose every outward and dental characteristic was that of a true roach, is bound to stir more controversy over other big roach. It was made known only this week that a 1964 roach of 3lb 14oz, equal to the British record set in 1938, had been confirmed as a true roach after a year-long probe. Yet experts have criticised this fish as a hybrid.

Now some anglers will be wondering if there is a true roach left in our fisheries. As Dr Keith Banister, of the Natural History Museum, said: 'This problem of roach hybrids is bound to grow worse in waters that already contain them. Their great weight comes from the bream side—but the more hybrid breeds, possibly with true roach, the less we will see of the bream characteristics.'

But that is a small consolation for Mr Whitehall, who dreamed of a glass-case specimen that was all his own work. Now he is back at work, stuffing big fish for other anglers at 11s an inch for coarse-skinned species and 13s 6d for smooth-skinned tench, trout and salmon. Glass cases extra, of course.

Mr Whitehall estimated the age of his fish by taking a magnified scale reading—rather like telling the age of a tree from the rings radiating from the centre of the trunk.

When it comes to underwater philandering the roach has plenty of competition from the unpretentious bleak. For this little chap has been known to flip a fin with chub, dace, rudd, roach and bream.

* * *

YORKSHIRE ANGLER Dennis Starling, a 38-year-old assistant export manager, tried his hand at sea fishing while holidaying near the estuary of the River Roe in Northern Ireland. And he caught a 12lb 2oz bass, a handsome specimen that many an expert, armed with the finest shore fishing tackle, would envy.

But Mr Starling caught his bass with an earthworm as bait, attached to a No. 8 freshwater hook, 8lb line, chain-store rod and a cheap 14s 6d reel.

I can almost hear the teeth gnashing in Redditch, Worcestershire, traditional home of British craftsman-made tackle. Be of good heart, gentlemen. It was surely high time to bury the hoary old tale about the small boy, bent pin and a stick. . . .

* * *

FOR TWO small boys, this week has brought the sort of angling baptism they will never forget. They may catch bigger fish . . . they may become famous competition anglers with showcases full of trophies.

But for eight-year-old John Popham, of Hertford, the memory of his struggle with a 3lb 3oz tench will remain unrivalled, no matter how many five-pounders may come his way later on.

And for five-year-old Christopher Taylor, of Wembley, the fearful excitement of hanging on to a rod that is connected to a powerful 27lb carp is a thrill many thousands of grown-up specimen hunters would like to share.

Both boys owe those memories to their fathers.

For Owen Popham, 42, went on a torchlit midnight crawl around his lawn to find the juicy lob-worms that tempted young John's tench in a lake at Nazeing, Essex. It was the best tench from the water for three years and came during the Hertford Angling Club's annual junior championships. But John had not entered for the contest and so missed his chance of the title.

I am willing to wager, however, that the story John had to tell when he went back to school next morning was worth a lost title. For his father's worm hunt also brought a bite from an even bigger tench—but the hook broke, the rod top cracked under the strain, and that was that.

As for little Christopher Taylor and his encounter with the huge carp—well, that is a fisherman's yarn in itself.

The carp was caught by his father, Tom Taylor,

on Monday afternoon after a quick dash to a gravel pit at Wraysbury, Buckinghamshire, when Christopher came out of school. The carp—the biggest so far this season—took a lump of crust floating 20ft from the bank on top of a weedbed, and tore more than 100 yards from the reel in its first plunging rush. Mr Taylor put on as much pressure as he dared with a 6lb line, but the carp reached the safety of thick weed and sulked for the greater part of two hours. And this is when excited young Christopher went to his father's aid, for Mr Taylor's landing net was damaged in his first attempt to net the fish. So Dad decided on a personal underwater confrontation.

Into the five-year-old's trembling hands went the 8ft fibreglass rod, while his father stripped and plunged into the lake to deal with the carp. Alone on the bank, Christopher held on to the bending rod, but suddenly shouted: 'Dad, it's pulling me in!'

Dad got to the carp first and brought it safely ashore . . . to set the phones ringing in Staines Angling Society's headquarters. The carp is a record for the club, beating the previous best of 25lb, caught only a week earlier.

*   *   *

THE SHARK lay in the bottom of the boat, its glistening length measured and remeasured by the anglers who stood around, recalling the breathless moments when the razor-toothed prize seemed certain to win its freedom. But the exhausted captor took no part in the angling shop-talk. He lay snugly wrapped and soundly asleep.

When you're only eleven years old and you have just fought and conquered a shark that is nearly twice your height and stronger than a man, it is so hard to stay awake when the reaction sets in. That is how it was last week for shark-catcher John Lister, the Brighton schoolboy who has qualified for membership of the exclusive Shark Angling Club of Great Britain—but under their rules he must wait for his fourteenth birthday before he can be admitted.

John's encounter with one of the World's most powerful fighting fish came during a Cornish holiday trip with his father, Mr Vince Lister, when Looe skipper Eric Brown took them out in his boat *Nautilus*.

Until the shark seized the mackerel bait, the boy's biggest thrill in previous sea-fishing trips had been a baby tope of 14lb. Those memories were swept away for ever as Mr Lister and Skipper Brown held on to the sides of John's chair and shouted instructions as the shark plunged and leapt

Arms full of ling is David Nunn, of Lanner, Redruth, Cornwall. Just 31lb 13oz at the weigh-in.

for a full half hour.

At the height of the struggle, Mr Lister tied a rope to the rear lugs of the big-game fishing reel to prevent the costly tackle from vanishing overboard. Then the skipper's gaff flashed expertly as John brought the beaten fish alongside. It was all over.

Five minutes later, the boy was fast asleep, worn out by a struggle that would have tested many a grown angler.

Meanwhile, back on the sunny beach, Mrs Brenda Lister sat in a deckchair, unaware that her only child was busily gaining a place in the record books as the only eleven-year-old to catch a 103lb blue shark. When she strolled along to the quay to rejoin her family, she was amazed to see her small son posing beside his catch. 'I never dreamed he would actually go and catch one,' she said.

It is no dream to young John. His most treasured possession is now the coveted green certificate issued by the Shark Club. And written on the back is John's name and address with the inscription: *Finder rewarded with 1s 6d.* That certificate, and the souvenir photographs taken at Looe, will be the talk of the first form at Brighton's De La Salle College next term.

For in addition to joining the ranks of the shark catchers—minimum qualifying weight for the Shark Club is 75lb—John has also passed his eleven-plus examination. And that, says his mother, was what she was really thinking about on the beach.

But I wouldn't be surprised if John lets his new schoolmates into a secret—the best shark his 'old man' has bagged this year is a mere tiddler of 65lb.

*   *   *

FOR EIGHTEEN years, angler Brian Wiseman has devoted most of his summer leisure to the pursuit of big tench. Patiently, skilfully he has built up his knowledge of *Tinca's* habits and haunts, gradually increasing the size of his successes.

Even a convalescence after an appendix operation was put to good use, producing his best tench of 7lb 5oz, a rare specimen that few anglers will ever have the luck to see.

The big 'uns come to everyone at some time, as Richard Wills' stories illustrate. Even chaps like Freddy, all of seven years old.

But, still not satisfied, Mr Wiseman took two weeks off work as a fork-lift operator at Marks Tey, near Colchester, Essex, and spent half of it holidaying with his wife and two-year-old daughter. The other half—his personal annual angling spree—came last week. And with it came his greatest success and cruellest disappointment.

In a lake only two-and-a-half miles from his home at Kelvedon, he hooked, landed and weighed the biggest tench ever caught in this country—an outsize fish of 9lb 2oz, beating the existing national rod-caught record by one ounce.

Shaking with excitement and worrying over the time the fish was being kept out of the water, Mr Wiseman carried it to his keepnet—and slipped on the rain-soaked bank.

Helplessly, despairingly he watched the greatest prize of an angling lifetime slip between his clutching fingers into the water . . . and glide away with a defiant flick of his giant 'spade' tail. No fish—no record.

Some I know would have quietly, but remorselessly, snapped their fishing rods over their knees, jumped up and down on the pieces and taken to drink. But not Mr Wiseman.

For one thing, two schoolboy anglers stood beside him stunned and overawed by what they had seen on the weighing scales. Also, there was still enough daylight left to cast a lump of bread paste on a No. 14 hook in the general direction of the departed record-breaker and pray for a miracle.

I would like to report that Mr Wiseman recaptured his dream fish. He deserved to. But Lady Luck, the fickle escort of all who go fishing, chuckled up her sleeve and sent him a mere four-pounder just before he packed up in the deepening dusk at 9 p.m.

For the suspicious ones who like to be reassured about such things, I report that Mr Wiseman's scales were checked by Steve Short, the well-known angling journalist, soon after the tench's brief visit and found to be accurate. And for those cheerful optimists who like to copy a successful tackle assembly on the happy assumption that what caught a 9lb 2oz tench in Essex is bound to be a dead cert in Yorkshire, here are the bits and pieces they need: Cane rod, 13ft long; 6lb line; fixed spool reel; size 14 hook to nylon; 8in quill float with four shots placed close to the hook; bread paste bait placed close to the lily pads.

You also need a 4ft deep, weedy swim that has not been fished much this season. See what I mean?

* * *

WHEN YOU are as big and powerful as a record tench, to regain your freedom after a fair fight is to brighten the gleam in the eyes of those who hunt you. But to be carelessly thrown back without anybody realising you are a record fish is shaming indeed.

That's what happened last weekend to a plump, 4½oz gudgeon caught in a River Severn match by Worcester official Bill Pritchard. The gudgeon was a ¼oz over the record, at present shared by three fish.

* * *

IF YOU still nurse the popular belief that angling is a peaceful, relaxing way to spend a few leisure hours, you should have a word with the customers in Mr Trevor Prince's off-licence at Catisfield, near Fareham, Hampshire. They know different.

This week, for example, his customers have noted that Mr Prince is limping around with a bandaged leg and a wrenched kneecap. Their practised eyes could not have failed to observe that his nose is twice its usual size. And that his usual cheery greeting is muffled by a swollen mouth and loosened front teeth.

But they don't worry about it. They know, from long experience, that Mr Prince's off-duty fishing trips are occasionally likely to leave him looking somewhat the worse for wear.

For Mr Prince has recently joined the select ranks of the shark hunters, and is proving highly successful at it. Already he is the proud holder of the British rod-caught record for porbeagle shark, with the huge 324lb specimen he captured a mile or two off the Isle of Wight last month—wresting the limelight from the traditional shark grounds off Looe, Cornwall.

His battered appearance this week follows a ninety-minute, no-holds-barred match with another heavyweight porbeagle which was only a few pounds lighter than the record fish. Mr Prince and his friend, Mr Dickie Downes, a local nurseryman, encountered the shark near the Nab Tower in the Solent.

They were about to pack their £300 worth of specialist tackle and turn back after a fishless day when the shark struck at the bait. That was when 30-year-old Mr Prince began to wonder if golf—dominoes, even—might not have been a less hazardous choice as a relaxing hobby.

Round One went to the shark as Mr Prince slipped and wrenched the knee he had strained the day before in stopping a dogfight near his shop.

Round Two was also a clear win for the shark, as Mr Prince took another long count on the deck with blood dripping from his nose. One of the gaff handles failed to open, and the plunging shark wrenched it from Mr Prince's grasp. Then the fish turned on its tail, and the swinging gaff handle struck the unhappy angler's nose—and also loosened most of his front teeth.

Round Three was a draw with one exhausted, bleeding, aching Mr Prince and the angry shark engaged in a tug-of-war that ended with the fish making another long run.

Round Four saw the gaffs driven home and the fish alongside. But it took three lengths of rope looped round its head, tail and middle, and the combined heave-ho of both anglers to get it on board. Then Mr Prince slipped on the wet decking and gashed a leg on an angle iron at the side of the boat.

They rode back to Fareham together—the victor to seek bandages, liniment and light duties; the vanquished to lie in state in a field at a discreet distance from the off-licence, to await collection by officials from Looe.

Yesterday Mr Prince, now one of the up-and-coming members of the Shark Angling Club, hobbled to the telephone to discuss how he felt after struggling with a 300lb shark for the length of time it takes to play a football match.

'The nearest equivalent I can think of,' he said, 'is to hang out of a bedroom window holding a hundredweight bag of cement, which someone has promised to take from you in two minutes but doesn't return for nearly two hours.'

* * *

THE BATHROOM scales at No. 28 Gore Road, Hackney, East London, are usually the feminine preserve of Mrs Doreen Freeman and her two daughters, Janet, 8, and Toni, 6. This applies also to the bath, in which the two little Freemans splashed happily, before their father, 27-year-old Mr Brian Freeman, gets home from work as a scaffolder.

But recently Mrs Freeman and her daughters found their bath and the scales taken over by an aggressive stranger in the form of an angry 30lb pike, nearly 4ft long. While the feminine Freemans peeped apprehensively round the bathroom door, the pike's proud captor was on the phone downstairs, asking the local tackle shop proprietor how much it would cost to transform the bath's temporary tenant into a mounted, glass-cased trophy.

'£40 at least,' came the answer. That quotation saved the life of the pike, and restored the bathroom to normal service.

Mr Freeman, who caught the pike on a 2s 6d day-ticket water at Cheshunt, Hertfordshire, decided the household budget was not geared to such luxuries as stuffed fish. Out came the plug in the bath, into a wet sack went the pike, and twenty minutes later the fish was carried from Mr Freeman's car to the banks of the gravel pit it has known so well for so many years.

A minute or so ticked by while the big fish recovered and then, with a flick of the huge tail, it swam off, unaware that only the high cost of expert stuffing had saved it from a permanent glassy-eyed stare.

Mr Freeman, who dabbled in sea fishing earlier this year because he was bored by freshwater sport, went to the pit for his first pike outing of the season. He caught a 4oz dace in a nearby stream and cast it out as live bait, attached to a size 6 treble hook and wire trace on a pike bung. The big pike took the dace so gently that Mr Freeman decided that it was a young 'jack' fish and offered his 10ft homemade rod to an angling friend, to help him gain experience.

Even while the offer was being refused, Mr Freeman spotted his capture swimming below the surface and thought his pipe dream of a twenty-pounder had come true. But weighed on the bank, the fish thumped a spring balance indicator to the 25lb limit and, obviously, was much heavier. It was then that Mr Freeman, aware that pike can live out of water for long periods, planned his car dash home, accompanied by the pike in a wet sack as a back-seat companion.

Weighed on the bathroom scales, which–as every angler's wife knows–are mercilessly accurate, the fish proved to be a true thirty-pounder, one of the best of the season. But the taxidermist had the last expensive word, and provided the Freeman schoolgirls with a fishy tale that is unlikely to be rivalled for some time to come.

For who, among the eight-year-olds, can cap a blood-curdling, true yarn of the day when a cold-eyed, toothy monster snapped and plunged in one's own bath?

The Duke of Bedford, a keen fisherman, casts an eye over the new lines in tackle at the National Angling Show.

*　*　*

TWELVE-YEAR-OLD Berkshire schoolboy Neil Benson has joined the elite corps of chub anglers with specimens of more than 5lb in their personal logbooks. Neil's rod-bender came from the Kennet and Avon Canal, near Newbury, last weekend in a return visit to a stretch which, a week earlier, produced a chub of 5lb 4oz 6dr for his father, Ken.

While Benson senior was settled hopefully in the same swim, young Neil chose a spot twenty yards away and cast in a lump of cheese paste. Twice the cry of 'Dad, I've got one!' fetched his father and a family friend from their swims with a landing net. But twice the hook pulled out and the grown-ups went back to their fishing point.

At Neil's third call they turned round to watch, waiting to see if their journey would be really necessary. Then they got to their feet in a hurry, for the boy was battling against long, steady runs that signalled a really good chub. On the bank, it weighed 5lb 4oz, a fraction of an ounce less than his father's capture.

All of which strikes a justifiably-proud note in Mr Benson's heart, and a disconcerting note in the hearts of most other angling dads. After all, there was a time when a 5lb chub meant secure paternal prestige for years. Now it's not even safe to assume that a piping call for the landing net is simply another whopping great gudgeon!

*　*　*

EVER SINCE Clarissa, the record 44lb carp, was hooked in a small, weedy Gloucestershire pool more than sixteen years ago–she was promptly transferred to a tank in the London Zoo–angling specimen hunters have spent patient, immobile days, nights and weeks at a time trying to go one better. No angler has tried harder, or more patiently, than Jack Hilton, a 41-year-old Hertfordshire landscape gardener, who took up the long, lone hunt for big fish ten years ago.

A self-confessed carp addict, Jack admits that only three men have succeeded in breaking through the 30lb carp barrier more than once. Fewer than

Awesome admirers of a typical blue shark, caught off the Cornish coast.

twenty-five carp in this heavyweight class have been caught, and one of these, a 35lb specimen, fell to Jack's rod last year.

So the odds against making Clarissa look small are long indeed. But it was towards her old home, in Redmire Pool, that Jack Hilton turned last year when he paid a fat fee to the owner for exclusive rights for himself and a few friends.

When the frosts came, he laid aside his carp rod until next season, and totted up the number of hours spent on his personal hunt at Redmire in 1968. They amounted to a fantastic total of 1,600 hours, or more than sixty-six days and nights, spread over mid-June to Autumn.

In late July he hooked and brought to his outsize landing net a carp so big that it lay across the arms of the net with inches to spare on either side. But

the fish remained rigid and shed the hook before it could be relaxed into the body of the net.

Says Jack: 'I'll never forget the sight of that huge shape sinking slowly out of sight. It was heartbreaking. But already we are making plans for next season, so wish us the best of skill, for we aren't looking for luck!'

One could be forgiven for thinking that a man who has clocked 1,600 fishing hours in the carp half of the season would look thankfully upon the long Christmas break as a chance to get his head down. Not Mr Hilton. To him, the cold winter months are best passed by catching big chub, bigger barbel and having a bash at the roach record for good measure.

That is why he is in the angling news again this week, less than a month after capturing an 11lb 6oz barbel. For Jack celebrated Christmas with a superb 2lb 12oz roach caught in the flooded Dorset Stour, on a tiny piece of legered bread crust.

* * *

MOST EVENINGS, electrical engineer Harry Taylor helps his wife, Roselie, to clear the supper dishes— then he settles down to running the affairs of Biggleswade Angling Club. His fourteen years' careful management has helped this Bedfordshire club to grow into a contented and influential organisation that provides good sport for more than 500 members.

And when it comes to the preparation of big matches, Harry and his match committee colleagues are masters of the art of handling the important details that make or mar any sizeable angling event.

So the arrangements for last weekend's annual 'special' on Biggleswade's stretch of the Great Ouse at Tempsford, to which eight clubs were invited, consumed many hours and weeks of Harry's leisure. With everything set for the big day, Harry dug for worms, prepared his own fishing tackle, bought 10s worth of best maggots, waved goodbye to his wife, and set off to enjoy his own part in the contest.

But within a couple of hours he was back home with the brief, simple and comprehensive announce-

And here comes another exciting capture for the Barrington-Martin picture album.

Fishing in the harbour at Carrickfergus, overshadowed by the historic castle.

ment heard at some time or other by so many anglers' wives and mothers: '*I FELL IN!*'

Not that Mrs Taylor really needed to be told. The puddles in the hall told their own story.

Harry's spectacular header into the swollen Great Ouse came after a rod-rest snapped and he slipped from the rain-soaked bank into deep water. Afterwards, 64-year-old Harry had a hot bath and survived his soaking without so much as a sniffle.

And he felt even better later when the match results were relayed to him—a fine win with a 34lb bag of good quality bream and roach by one of his own members.

All Harry needs now to put him on top of the world again is for someone to hook his lucky, wool fishing hat which swirled away during his ducking. The hat was a gift from his wife on a Norfolk fishing holiday eight years ago. He wore it on every fishing trip, his Biggleswade badge glinting proudly on the front.

On Sunday, the Biggleswade anglers will be out in force along the Great Ouse, fishing in a match against Northampton. For both teams the quarry will be the river's plump bream and handsome roach—and Harry Taylor's little woolly hat.

Harry, sitting well back from the edge, will be out there with them. But hoping that his catch will end up on his head and not, for once, in his keepnet.

*　　*　　*

SCARFACE the pike is undisputed king of the Middlesex lake* in which it has lived and grown old during a fattening reign of terror. Battle after battle has been fought and won against small boys, specimen hunters and old men, who sighed over their broken tackle but relished the telling of the tale.

In the telling, Scarface grew to such tremendous proportions that only a hushed whisper was fit for the description of the huge jaws, the cold eyes that gleamed from the depths and the glimpses of the hook scars that ran across the gill coves. And no arms could stretch wide enough to do justice to the size of the monster whose mighty body broke free with such contemptuous ease.

So, like many other fishermen's yarns, the fish became something of a half-believed legend and even the privileged few who jousted and lost in those underwater tournaments began to wonder if their memories played them false.

Then, last Sunday, along the banks of the lake came the angler whose skill could match the old pike's tricks, whose wrists could master the plunging fury—an angler fit to receive the honourable

The holiday angler legers a deep run by the far bank for chub.

surrender of Scarface the pike.

Gentlemen, the toast is Susan Campbell, a pretty, 21-year-old slip of a girl from Wembley, who took up fishing only a couple of years ago but, today, could be hailed as the new holder of the British pike record if . . .

That 'if' is the all-important records committee rule which requires the body of the fish, dead or alive. But as Susan, her boy friend Gordon Hiscock and other male witnesses of this remarkable feminine triumph could not find suitable weighing scales, they measured Scarface carefully from nose to tail and then returned the elderly warrior to the water—unaware that the only freshwater pike record ever to be held by a woman might be slipping through their fingers.

For Scarface measured exactly 4ft 6in, with a girth of 22in. And according to Mona's weight-for-length scale, a pike of this size should weigh 49lb. This compares with the best English pike of 40lb, captured by Norfolk poultry farmer Peter Hancock in 1967, and the Loch Lomond pike of 47lb 11oz which was struck from the record lists only a few weeks ago.

Susan and Scarface came face to face after an epic struggle that lasted ten minutes in a swim 15ft deep and ended with Gordon and two other men slipping and sliding down a steep, muddy bank to cope with a landing net that threatened to collapse. Then, still in the net, Scarface was attached to a spring balance that jolted to its 25lb limit mark and broke.

While Susan—a dental nurse at Sudbury, Middlesex—kept a professional but wary eye on the dog-sized teeth, a gag was inserted to open the pike's mouth for removal of the snap tackle hooks. But the huge jaws crunched the metal gag like tinfoil and a stronger gag had to be found. A second snap tackle, hanging from the gaping mouth in evidence of an earlier victory for Scarface, was also removed.

Susan is no fair-weather angling-picnic companion. She and Gordon belong to their firm's angling club. They go fishing almost every weekend and concentrate on pike in the winter months.

Her account of pike strategy is as cool and professional as any tough, male specimen hunter. 'Conditions were ideal—fairly cold but clear and sunny with a slight breeze . . . ideal pike weather,' she reports crisply.

And of Scarface's entry into her angling life she says simply: 'I cast out a dead sprat on Jardine snap tackle and waited a full two hours for a run. Then the main and pilot floats moved away towards deeper water and I struck, steering the fish away from a clump of reeds. I was flabbergasted when I saw how big it was.'

Susan's boy friend smiled manfully and said: 'After years of trying to catch a double-figure pike, I feel like giving up.' And the young reporter who interviewed shapely Susan returned to declare: 'She's the dishiest pike angler I've ever seen!'

Jack Hargreaves, the famous TV angling personality, with everything at the ready—including pipe.

Sorry, pike fans, I cannot disclose the exact location of the lake. It is controlled by the London Anglers' Association and Susan would land in trouble if she broke their rules about Press reports.

IT'S A FAR CRY...

. . . from the shivering waters of snowbound Britain. Actually, the setting is the Pohangina River, in the North Island of New Zealand. A nice catch in any island, we say.

All about...

HOOKS

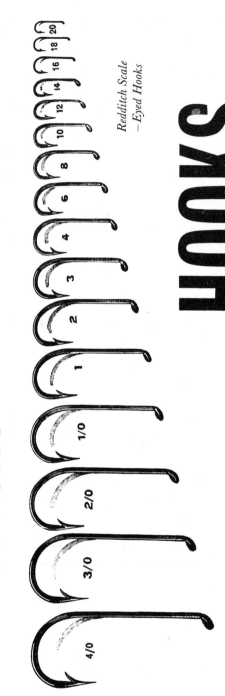

*Redditch Scale
– Eyed Hooks*

BRITISH fish-hook makers produce hundreds of millions of hooks every year – and eighty per cent of these are exported.

Each country has its own special requirements and in the last hundred years or so, British manufacturers have been obliged to supply more than 10,000 distinct styles, shapes and sizes of hooks.

But most of the hooks made for use in Britain are supplied in a handful of styles – *Model Perfect, Octopus Point, Sproat, Crystal and Standard Treble.

The Redditch Scale of fish hook sizes is used all over the World, and the life-size sketches on this page illustrate the scales for Eyed Hooks and Crystal Hooks.

NOTE: For your interest, the full scale originally designed for Crystal Hooks is shown, but nowadays only the even sizes below size 6 are made, i.e. 8, 10, 12, 14, etc.

*Model Perfect is the trade mark of S. Allcock and Co. Ltd., and Octopus Point is the trade mark of Edgar Sealey and Sons, Ltd.

*Redditch Scale
– Crystal Hooks*

With acknowledgements to National Angling Show data produced by the British Craftsmanship Guild.

68

John Neville

A PRACTICAL APPROACH TO FLY FISHING

JOHN NEVILLE is a well-known figure in Sheffield, city of fishing fanatics. He does both coarse and fly fishing, but is probably better known for his skills with the fly rod. He writes for several angling papers and is a gifted teacher of fly fishing.

I WAS twelve when I had my first day of fly fishing, and the water I chose was an old canal where maggot fishing for roach was more fitting than casting a fly. Yet the events of that day are still clearly etched in my memory.

I smile to myself when I recall the tackle I used for this first attempt. An old roach rod with a big wooden reel, together with a thick, undressed sea line and my one and only fly (a huge red tag), were the best attempt at fly tackle that I could muster.

Anglers, fishing nearby for tackle-shy roach, shuddered visibly as I waved that incongruous outfit wildly in the air and made my first cast. The fly landed among yards of tangled line and gut, but a fair-sized chub (seeming enormous to my youthful eyes) immediately rose and hooked itself on the fly.

Many years have passed since that lucky day, and I have become hooked firmly on the drug-like addiction that is fly fishing. A moderate amount of success has come my way on fly, with fish of many kinds from many varied waters, but the greatest pleasure I have had from fly fishing isn't connected with personal triumphs at all.

Nothing equals the thrill I have had from teaching other people to fly fish, especially youngsters who get a real kick out of catching even a small

69

MEET THE RAINBOW MAN...

His name is Barrie Welham, and he is managing director of Garcia Tackle Ltd—which means that his whole life is all about fishing. Here Mr Welham lines up five rainbows taken from Two Lakes (Hampshire), three on dry fly.

Total weight: 17lb 8oz. On the opposite page, he holds a 5lb 10oz trout which he took on a small brown nymph from the same waters, and the picture below is proof of his prowess as a salmon fisher.

fish on fly. With a little assistance from me, many people have discovered the delights of fly fishing—among them old men, boys, and ladies—but my most rewarding attempt at tuition resulted from a chance meeting.

On my way to work one evening, I passed a young angler struggling up a steep hill with a fishing basket on his back and I offered him a lift in the van.

Soon I discovered that my companion didn't even know that it was the close season for coarse fishing, and that the only fish he should have been seeking just then were trout.

He told me that he would like to fish for trout, especially with fly tackle, but he thought it would prove too difficult and too expensive for him. There and then I made a rather rash promise that I would teach him to fly fish, and see to it that he caught some trout.

A few days later, in the local tackle shop, I helped him to choose a fly-fishing outfit comprising rod, reel and line. To his surprise, the whole lot cost less than £6.

Immediately, he insisted on practising casting on the lawn at home, and I watched him making all the mistakes of the beginner in his eagerness to get on with it.

Like a sergeant-major, I drilled him hard and pointed out again and again his faults. 'You are taking the rod too far back on the back cast,' I yelled, and 'Your wrist is breaking back instead of staying rigid.'

I tried for hours to cure his weak, sloppy back casts, for which he tried to compensate by a hard forward cast. 'Remember,' I said, 'it's like a dance time on the back cast . . . *slow, quick, STOP.*'

'Say to yourself all the time: *Hard* back and gently forward.'

My young friend showed a determination I had never before come across, and he practised hard every day for months on end. Besides picking my brains, he sought out others who could help him and he read every book in his local library that dealt with fly fishing.

He begged me to teach him also the rudiments of fly tying, and he started to swot up on this subject at every spare moment.

John Neville is pictured here fly fishing in a remote Scottish loch.

He asked for, and received, a free casting lesson from the great Charles Ritz at the Game Fair, and he pestered Geoffrey Bucknall for fly-tying tips at the National Angling Show.

In no time, it seemed, we fished together for a few days on the lovely little River Llugwy in Wales, seeking the small, wild trout that are so common there.

At once it became apparent that my pupil had applied himself really well to his practising. Throughout the first day he matched me fish for fish, taking trout after trout as though he had been at it for many years instead of only a few months – and that on grass instead of water.

He astonished me by casting to, and catching, a trout that rose a good 18 yards away beneath an overhanging tree branch. All the time he gave the impression of utter competence.

Many other fish were taken that first season, including some fine rainbows from the Derbyshire Wye and lots of brownies from an overgrown little brook. However, the technique of wet fly fishing on still waters seemed to elude him, and it was not until halfway through his second season that success came his way in this kind of fishing. He surprised me on this occasion, too.

After flogging away for hours without a single take, just as he had done so many times before, he began to wind in his line as fast as possible, saying: 'Oh, hang it, I'm going to fish round the other side of the pond.' Hardly were the words out of his mouth than his rod kicked violently and he was into a fish. Actually it turned out to be *two* fish, both fair-sized trout, and both were landed!

From that day to this, he has never had any trouble catching trout on wet fly!

Now, after a mere three seasons at the game, he has beaten many good anglers by taking second place in an open trout fly-casting competition, and he ties flies that are the equal of any that I have seen.

It helps to be a left-hander with a cast like this. Charles Derrick fishing the 5s-per-day Driffield Canal. Fly only on this stretch.

He even teaches fly tying to night-school pupils and thus offsets some of his fishing expenses.

I have told you this true story to illustrate that it does not take years of experience to become a competent fly fisher.

Remember that many of the old hands who tend to scoff at the youngsters, and boast of the fact that they have fished 'man and boy for over 40 years,' are only casual anglers. Some of them fish only once a month at the most.

Alan, for that is my young friend's name, put in more effort in two years than many an angler does in a lifetime.

To anyone thinking of taking up fly fishing I would give the following advice:–

SEEK expert help with the casting at first, then put in half-an-hour's practice a day for several months.

LEAVE the more difficult branch of fly fishing with wet fly on still water alone at first, and try dry fly on a good river.

GO in that most rewarding period of the year, the end of May and the beginning of June, for your first attempt at fishing, and try to get an experienced fly fisher to accompany you.

ALWAYS carry a slip of oilstone to sharpen your fly hooks, for most shop flies are on blunt hooks. Remember that the most common cause of failure is not using the wrong fly but scaring the fish.

ALWAYS be prepared to cast from a kneeling or sitting position rather than standing up. And approach the water with caution.

IGNORE entomology at first. Use a light-coloured fly such as a 'coachman' on bright days, and a dark fly like the 'black gnat' in dull weather.

REMEMBER that a fish caught on a fly of your own tying gives twice as much pleasure as one on a shop-bought fly.

IF permits for top-class trout waters seem expensive, economise on other items. Do without fancy fly boxes, amadou fungus to dry your fly, and special oil to make it float. Use instead tobacco tins, paper tissues, and medicinal paraffin.

SEEK expert help, and practice, practice, practice. Then practice more.

Alan often says that the day he met me changed his whole life. Maybe this article will start *you* off on a lifetime of fly fishing pleasure.

A fine trout from the River Wharfe at Arthington, for Mr Horace Longman's bag.

Beauty . . . tranquillity . . . a lone visitor from Llanberis fishing in Llyn Padarn, with Llanberis Castle and the Snowdon range in the background.

TOM WILLIAMS

Tom Williams comes from a family of gamekeepers and his first job, at the age of fourteen, was working on an estate in Lancashire. He then became gamekeeper on a Berkshire estate through which the River Kennet runs. Later he was a head river keeper on the famous River Itchen for five years. Tom is now fishery manager on the Earl of Radnor's Longford Estate in Hampshire with six miles of main river, six miles of chalk stream and some eighteen miles of main carrier under his control.

MY COUNTRY LIFE

THE poets of old must have been anglers all, for surely this 'Oh, to be in England' stuff was inspired by green meadows and clear running water.

When that first feeling of warmth creeps into the air at the end of winter, the river slowly comes out of its austere garb and starts to live. The water meadow grasses grow lush as a warming current from the stream is fed into the fields.

Grannum ride in the surface eddies, struggling to get airborne before the dace and grayling can take them as part of their first surface feed of the year; in the small back eddies under the bank, the chub shoal on the surface sip in an easy meal. Everything starts to happen at once.

The first bright greens on the willows are bordered by bright, yellow patches of kingcups in the meadows behind. The early migrants fly in from warmer continents. The first swallow twists his way upstream, not caring to stop while the warmth in the wind pushes him on.

In the bowl of a pollarded willow, the bitch mink gives birth to five blind, hairless and helpless cubs. The mother, a third generation bred in the wild from an original escapee of the local mink farm, has not yet learned the necessity of being cautious in her daily life. She hunts the river bank among the young of the duck and moorhen, and pays little heed to the passing farmhand. This unafraidness will prove her end before the year moves far.

These warm spring winds bring with them the rain and the March dust is laid to colour up the falling water of the river, as up from the sea, with the scent of the spate in his nostrils, comes the magnificent spring salmon. The angler who has fished for him since the first of February now catches a first glimpse of his quarry as he lifts himself out of the water with a sudden urge to be gone to the upper reaches. In the deep slack holes under the bank, the roach shoal with the perch to share a joint place of spawning.

This is a busy time for the keeper, an eye must be

kept on each beat to see that every trout or salmon rod does not lack for a few words of encouragement; at the same time, the grass cutter must be out and the first surge of spring growth taken off the bank. That litter of mink cubs must be spotted by working out more or less the central part of the bitch's hunting area. There are fish to be weighed and photographed and, not the least, to be toasted in the local hostelry, one of the more pleasant duties that normally means a happy end to a spring day.

Still the temperatures rise, and the nymphs are quickly maturing on the river bed until, at some unknown signal (perhaps a joining of air and water temperatures), they head for the surface to hatch as 'iron blues' or 'large dark olives'.

The mayfly decides to join in the general rush to be up and out of this water, and in those moments before she has completely struggled out of her snuck she runs the gauntlet of every surface feeding fish in the river. Some survive to be picked off by the hawking chaffinch, or to be taken with an audible thump by the swift as it hurtles on its feeding run.

At no time is the river valley more bountiful than this part of the year. The shallows and cattle drinks abound with dace fry that are fed on by last year's trout, and the kingfisher gathering feed for its brood buried deep in the bank of the neighbouring stream.

The otter has turned her attention, and that of her cubs, to the packed chub, who have been cleaning themselves in the fast water; the bitch mink takes an unending toll of the young mallard who are unable to fly to escape her persistent chase. The roach, discoloured by the garb they clothed themselves in for spawning, gather in the fast water behind the hatches and clean themselves for the coming year.

Time slips by. The early spring salmon, undiscovered by searching baits, grows stale in a deep hole under the willow. Parasites in his gills irritate him into movement so that he surges forward from his lie and hurtles into the air, and like a stone skipping the surface repeats his leap, diminishing to a show of his tail as he turns to go back to his hole and his ruminating stillness.

There is an excitement about the river banks and

This is the enviable country life of Tom Williams – and his ever-ready gun dogs.

in my cottage, for the middle of the year has brought the coarse fisherman back to the riverside. While the salmon angler still walks the bank, now searching for the smaller summer fish, he walks round and past the fishing stool, ground bait bags and the pleasant character of the other angler.

The grass is long again and for a third, or fourth, time it must be cut, but now the machine has the added hazards of late nests along the bank, of rodrests and keepnets left by the careless or uncaring.

And so to August and the doldrums of the fishing year, with the water so clear that the bed of the river, no matter its depth, is shown. The fish from the sea have grown stale and refuse even to lift when disturbed by passing lines.

The coarse fish bury themselves in a profusion of weedy channels, refusing to be lured by baits on lines that are plain to see. But this is the holiday period and our fishermen must fish, for at this time they bring their wives to see their pleasures of the winter months. They knit and nod and while away a time and shout to Johnny down the bank, while a single dace means success where they would have been unsatisfied a few short weeks ago.

Gradually leaves grow old on trees, and as they turn to colours gold, they splash the scene to steal the year's delight from spring.

The eel finds a restlessness in his search for food, his hunger departs, his coat changes from a muddy brown to a bright silver. His stomach closes and ceases to need its mighty stream of food. Then, in the dark of the month, when the moon is obscured and the recent rain has put that tinge of colour from the fields into the water, some instinct sends him downstream to the sea, there to join those from other streams before heading for the breeding ground in the deeps.

He was not alone in waiting for this time. The eel traps had been carefully repaired, their slatted floors have been tested, and hatches made to lift. On this ideal night of wind and rain, the keeper in his trap gathers a fishy harvest for the jellied eel stalls of London and Midlands towns.

Along the river banks, the first frosts lay an early-morning carpet of white, revealing animals' tracks that used it as a highway in the night. A muddy patch, a scuffled area, shows where the otter emerged to shake her coat. Her area has been diminishing to concentrate within a few hundred yards up and downstream of the holt, and suspicion says that she is on the point of dropping an autumn litter.

With the weed now gone and a little rain flowing straight into the river, the season is right for deceiving fish. The natural abundance of earlier months has finished, wisdom has grown among the lowly nymphs and shrimps in their need for survival. The baited hook is carried fast downstream, and fish must decide within a moment if they should eat or let it go.

The lordly salmon has lost his silver coat, and has changed his deep and healthy look to that of spawning garb. Under the shelter of the leafless

A nice chub is landed—and there's no need for a net, either!

A BONNIE PLACE TO FISH

This is what fishing is all about, say the Scots. Our picture from Dumfriesshire shows the River Annan, its level raised to a good fishing height by heavy rains.

Tom Williams fishes a stretch of the many miles of water under his control.

trees, where the river runs fast over bright and polished gravel, the hen salmon digs her redd and buries her eggs. On the tail of the redd, the coarse fish gather to glean those eggs that escape being buried.

Then into the new year and coarse fishing at its best. The drab scene along the banks is brightened by the green umbrellas and the quiet business of the expert anglers.

Winter floods scour the river bed, altering its pattern wherever a weakness is found, undermining banks and dropping the earth and clay into the river. New back eddies are formed, where pike shelter from the pace of the current and wait for shoals of unwary dace to be driven in.

Debris from the upper reaches washes down, blocking hatchways and clogging weed racks. Oil drums and footbridges, dead sheep and fences, all pushed on by the rising water. In these conditions the dace spawn, and handle rough to the hand on their way into the keepnet.

While the coarse fisherman drags out every last moment from the end of the season, the salmon angler starts again to look for his early fish; for a short while the two anglers share the water, each in his own way sure of the nuisance of the other. But when evening comes and rods are broken down and there are fish to be admired, the 2lb roach and the 20lb salmon each takes a full share of its moment of glory.

PETER WHEAT

...GIVING SOME EXPERT ADVICE TO

The Newcomer

to Angling

PETER WHEAT has fished in many parts of the World and is well-known for his fishing articles. He was Editor of the old Anglers World *magazine. His favourite species are chub and barbel and he has taken chub to 5lb 8oz and barbel to 12lb 7oz.*

THE first requirement for any newcomer to angling is a suitable outfit with which to catch fish.

It is possible to achieve some success using nothing more imposing than a garden cane, a length of strong thread and a hook; indeed, as a youngster I gained a great deal of pleasure catching tiddlers with just such an outfit. Nevertheless, to get involved in angling and stand a reasonable chance of catching fish consistently (including a few big ones) requires proper tackle.

The modern tackle shop is a bewildering place. Rods, reels, landing nets and all manner of equipment line the walls and shelves, and initially at least, it is impossible to select what you need without some helpful advice. If you have a knowledgeable angling friend then enlist his services; otherwise, seek out a tackle shop of good reputation and get the dealer to advise.

Freshwater fishing has three main followings:—
Game angling involves the pursuit of salmon,

REEL POSITIONS

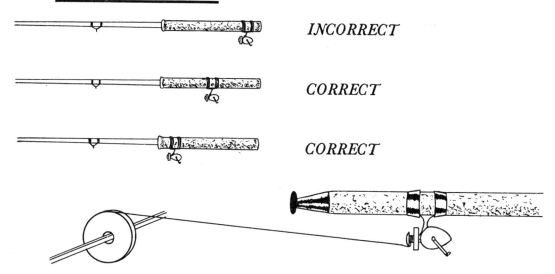

INCORRECT

CORRECT

CORRECT

Winding a line from the plastic spool to the line drum.

brown trout, rainbow trout and sea trout, using artificial flies, spinners, plugs, lures and small fish.

Match angling concerns the catching of coarse fish in competitions of various kinds, for individual and team awards, employing float and leger methods.

Coarse fishing, pure and simple, is the approach favoured by the majority, and this is where the newcomer must make his start. With an understanding of all coarse-fish methods, one is perfectly able to catch fish in matches, and also seek salmon and trout, but this ability takes time to develop and it would be unwise to try everything at once.

The first purchase of tackle should include the essential items for float and leger fishing, and just a few important accessories which one should never be without. So let us make a start with the rod.

Rods are constructed from several materials: cane (either whole or from split sections), fibreglass (both hollow and solid), and tubular steel. I firmly suggest that a first rod should be in hollow fibreglass. Such a weapon is lightweight, strong, and requires little attention to preserve its long-lasting qualities.

Length is important. Years ago, float rods were

long and leger rods short, but these days one can buy a rod suitable both for float fishing and legering – although some compromise must always be made. For instance, there are waters where a rod with a length of 13-14ft is a decided advantage, but again such a rod would be quite unsuitable for legering, say, a fast river like the Hampshire Avon.

The ideal first rod should have a length of between 10ft and 11ft with an action – that is to say, the shape of the bend when the rod top is pulled over – extending in a smooth arch through the top two-thirds. Like all rods, this general purpose type may have two or three sections. I doubt if it matters greatly, but I prefer a two-section rod, with or without a detachable butt for ease of carrying.

Rod rings are often subject to grooving following extensive fishing due to line friction, and as this could cause a cut or frayed line while under pressure from a big fish, it pays to ensure that the rod rings are of good quality. I favour rings of stainless steel with a hard chrome finish or, for butt and tip rings especially, ones with pink-coloured Syntox linings.

To assemble a rod with three sections, the top section is first fitted into the middle section, and then the butt section added – making sure all the rings line up and the fit is firm. In the case of metal ferrules, this may be too tight so that the male part cannot be pushed right home. The cause is often a build-up of dirt on the ferrule, which can be removed with a brass or silver cleaning fluid.

Should the fit still be unsatisfactory, a light rub with a fine grade emery-paper will do the trick – but it must be done with absolute care to avoid the removal of any more surface than is necessary.

The most versatile of the reels for coarse fishing is the fixed-spool. It may look a bit complicated at first, but with a little instruction from the tackle dealer you will be able to master the basic technique in a short time. Casting with the fixed-spool is quite easy, and even very long casts can be made with pinpoint accuracy.

Reels are rarely satisfactory for casting or playing fish if they are mounted close to the bottom of the handle. The more suitable position is at least the centre, or better still, a few inches down from the shoulder.

Lines for coarse fishing are mainly of nylon monofilament. The line drums for fixed-spool reels are detachable, which allows for a selection of lines to be carried and interchanged quickly as required. Monofilament is purchased, usually in 100yd spools, according to breaking strain. It is a good idea to carry two fixed-spool line drums, one loaded with 3lb breaking strain and the other with 5lb breaking strain.

To transfer a line from its plastic spool to the line drum, the reel is mounted back-to-front on the rod butt, the end of the line knotted firmly to the drum, and the bale-arm engaged. A friend will be needed at this stage to control the line as it leaves the spool.

If it is left to peel off any-old-how, you will be winding in twists and turns which can be an absolute menace when fishing. Your friend puts a pencil through the hole in the line spool and then, with a hand pressed either side of the spool, gripping the pencil, he applies pressure enough to tense the line between spool and drum.

Don't wind the line on too fast or your friend could get a nasty skin burn! Fill each drum evenly with line almost to the lip as an aid to smooth casting.

The quality of the line is obviously an important

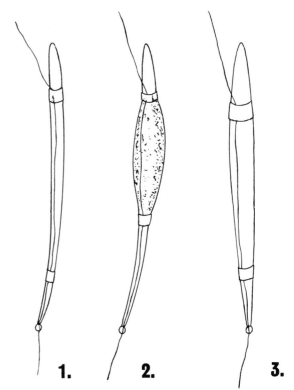

Here are three suitable floats: 1. Quill, 2. Quill with cork body, 3. Plain balsa float.

consideration, so choose a make with a high reputation for reliability. All monofilament has one drawback – it sometimes loses strength very quickly, irrespective of age or make. To guard against trouble of this kind, check the breaking strain regularly against the pull of a spring balance, and change all line at least once each season.

For float fishing, purchase just a small selection of floats. Quills of various sizes are quite cheap and suitable for a wide range of fishing, and quills with cork bodies are also useful, as are plain balsa floats.

Don't bother at this stage with any of the fancy, specialised patterns. They have their uses, which you will learn about as you progress, but to start with, plain simple floats are the best.

To attach a float, buy a few lengths of rubber tubing such as are used for aeromodel fuel pipes. With the line threaded through all the rings, two quarter-inch lengths of tubing are passed up the line. The top one is pushed over the head of the

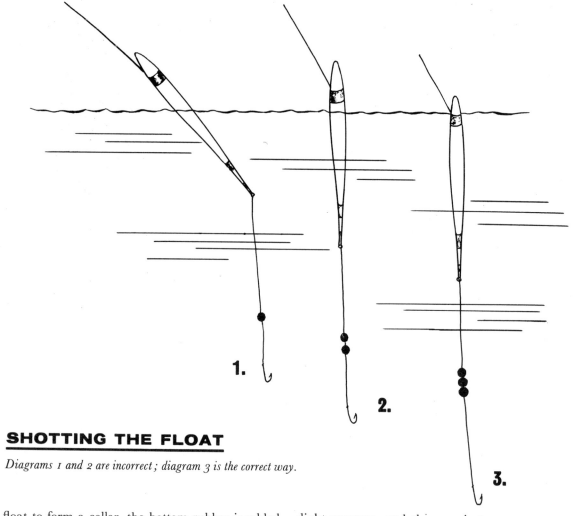

SHOTTING THE FLOAT

Diagrams 1 and 2 are incorrect; diagram 3 is the correct way.

float to form a collar, the bottom rubber is added likewise to the base. If the rubbers make a firm, tight fit, the float is adequately secure, but if you wish, the line can then be threaded through the small wire eye.

To make the float cock in the water and stand upright with just the minimum of tip protruding above the surface, split shot are added to the line. These are small balls of lead with splits down their sides, and they can be bought in various sizes. The three main ones are: AAA, BB, and swanshot—the largest of all. An ounce of each will last a very long time.

Avoid the hard, shiny black shot which take considerable pressure to press on the line and will often crush and weaken it considerably. Soft shot, which have a dull grey colour, can be attached with only

slight pressure, and they are just as easy to open again for removal.

Some anglers mount their shot in patterns to help with the better presentation of the bait, but personally I don't believe it matters very much, providing the tail—the distance between hook and bottom shot—is at least six inches.

Finally you need hooks, which can be bought, rather expensively, attached to lengths of nylon monofilament, or loose with either an eye or spade end for attachment direct to the main line. Of all three types I much prefer eyed hooks, which are cheap and, when attached direct to the line, cut out the weakness of extra knots.

The tie to use is called the Domhof knot, tied this way: Take the hook between forefinger and thumb of the right hand so that the eye protrudes beyond the tips, then with the left hand pass the end of the line through the eye and along the shank. Now bring it back in a loop and take the line several times round the shank, finally passing the end through the loop.

Very carefully, by pulling on the standing part of the line above the eye, work everything tight against the shank, and nip off the waste end. The result is a neat whipping knot of great reliability.

Hooks are bought according to numbered sizes – the higher the number the smaller the hook.

I suggest a range including the following sizes will cover most needs: 16, 14, 12, 8, 6, 4. A hook size is chosen to suit the size of the bait being used – maggots, 16, 14, 12; bread paste, 12, 8; lobworms, 8, 6; large cheese cubes and paste balls, 6, 4.

A leger rig is just as easy to fix up. The weights can be bought in a range of types and sizes. Two popular patterns are Arlesey Bombs and Bullet Weights, but probably the best of all is constructed from 2in lengths of monofilament and a number of swanshot.

Bend the nylon, which should be a lower breaking strain than the reel line, in a loop and secure both parts together with a swanshot to form a small eye through which the line is threaded.

When legering, the tackle lies right on the bottom, and the tail, in this case from hook to leger stop, is set at from 1ft to 18in. This distance is reduced to two or three inches when using a buoyant bait like bread crust.

A leger stop, which prevents the leger from running right down to the hook, can be a small split shot, but the latest type is the plastic plug stop which can be bought in packets of a dozen. In this case, a tiny plastic tube is threaded up the line and held in position with a tapering plug.

After the hook has been attached as before, the swanshot leger can be adjusted according to fishing conditions. For instance, extra shot can be added

to the nylon tails to hold bottom in a fast river, or to aid long casting when required in wide rivers and lakes.

Fishing for small growing species like roach, rudd and dace, the 3lb line will be suitable; for larger fish, chub, barbel, tench and small carp and pike, the 5lb line is best. Very big carp and pike are fish

HOOKS

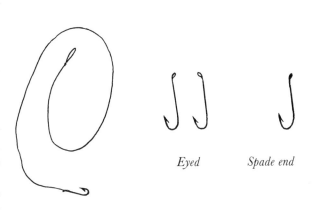

Eyed   *Spade end*

To nylon

more suited to the specialist and, in fact, require special tackle.

Accessories for anglers are numerous but by no means necessary, apart from just two which, in my opinion, are as essential as the tackle for catching fish.

One of these is a large landing net with an extending handle, required for netting out fish

DOMHOF KNOT

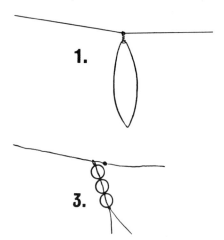

1.

3.

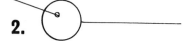

2.

LEGER WEIGHTS

1. Arlesey bomb.
2. Bullet leger.
3. Swanshot link leger.

Peter Wheat controls a large fish to the bank. Peter Stone stands by with the net.

above 8oz and particularly valuable if you hook a big one, as most anglers do from time to time.

The other item is a disgorger for removing hooks from fish hooked too far back for removal with the fingers. There are several types, but the best by far is an artery forceps disgorger with serrated teeth and a locking action.

Once the forceps have been clamped in position over the hook shank, it becomes a simple matter to work the hook loose without causing any damage to the delicate organs of the fish. Care of the catch and their safe return is the primary concern of every angler.

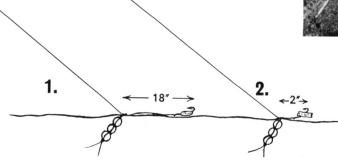

1.   ← 18″ →   **2.**   ←2″→

'TAIL' DISTANCES: *1. Normal baits; 2. Buoyant baits.*

PLASTIC PLUG LEGER STOP

Not the sort of fishing to be recommended for fair-weather sailors ! A rough day afloat in a Norwegian fjord.

SITTING.. STANDING.. CASTING

SITTING it out at Brighton (left) . . . and a far cry from the goings-on seen on the previous page!

STANDING, and full of youthful hopes and ambitions, is this line-up of boys at Southend (below opposite).

CASTING into a cold, grey sea (right) is this well-clad enthusiast on Saltburn Pier.

WAITING and hoping, on the catwalk at the mouth of the River Arun (below), from which bass to 10lb are caught.

AITING.. ON PIER AND CATWALK

CARP
FISHING

by Jack Hilton

THE AUTHOR is one of the best-known carp anglers in Britain, with fish of 35lb and 28¾lb to his credit. During the summer of 1968, he spent 1,600 fishing hours in search of a new British carp record. Jack, who is a landscape gardener, was founder of the former Hertfordshire Specimen Group and started his personal hunt for big fish ten years ago.

To the true carp addict there is only one carp worthy of attention — the LARGEST!

TO a devout carp enthusiast no other branch of fishing is equal to the pursuit of carp, that tough and worthwhile adversary whose elusiveness is legendary on some of the waters which hold really big specimens. But the long, often inactive days and nights spent at the waterside have a special attraction, seemingly of another world, where a lifetime can appear too short for the task in hand.

Yet, fortunately for the man with limited time at his disposal, there are two almost distinct kinds of carp fishing.

In one, success is measured by carp caught in excess of 10lb (and fish of lesser weight are rarely acceptable) and these fish can provide enough sport for the angler to remain of sound mind!

These days there are many waters which are suitable for this kind of carp fishing. The fishery to be looked for here is the type termed 'hungry', often of fair acreage (but not necessarily), yet with a good head of carp in proportion to its size. Rarely do carp from 'hungry' waters attain weights much in excess of 15lb or so, and once the basic principles of carp fishing have been mastered, only a modicum of common sense is required to catch fish fairly regularly.

But to the true carp addict there is only one carp worthy of attention–the LARGEST fish he knows of! This love of the sport can become a way of life, almost to the extent of becoming an obsession, but the reward when a big carp comes rolling to the net makes all the long, weary and often frustrating hours well worth the effort.

For make no mistake about it, the larger the carp sought, the more effort that is required in its capture. The men who choose to pit their wits and time, and spare themselves so little in the pursuit, do so in a way that can be imagined only vaguely by the average angler.

Let us assume the aim of such men is to capture a carp weighing 30lb or more. A surprising number of waters are capable of producing fish of this weight, but at the time of writing fewer than 25 carp of this calibre have yet been caught, and only three men have ever succeeded in breaking through the 'barrier' more than once.

One of these men caught the monster of 44lb from Redmire Pool in the dark hours of one September morn in 1952. His fish has held the carp record to this day and he needs no introduction from me – Richard Walker, who has possibly done more than any other to lift the veil of mystery that previously surrounded carp angling.

On the more difficult waters, it is uncanny the way carp can ignore the most tasty morsel as bait, or even as a free offering. Their ability to recognise the danger provided by the angler is almost unbelievable. They can and do learn not only from their own mistakes but from those of their brethren, and the apparent success of a particular bait can be very short-lived indeed.

I could give many examples of this behaviour pattern, but the most obvious that springs to mind is the way carp react to floating crust baits. When first fished for in this manner they will, if in any kind of feeding mood, take in a most confident way. Cruising slowly along they stop to poise gracefully below the offering, taking it with one enormous gulp that makes one's heart perform acrobatics! But what a marked difference when numbers of fish have been caught by this method – they soon learn to view such baits with caution!

They will cruise repeatedly around and below the crust, swirling and slurping, sometimes rushing towards the bait at breakneck speed only to 'come short' at the last split-second. If the bait becomes detached from the hook during these antics then often it will be taken along with other free offerings, although other hook-baits may be ignored.

Eventually, the time arrives when even free offerings are not taken, but long before this state of affairs is reached it is advisable for the carp fisher to try a new bait or method – or both. Perhaps, in later seasons, a return to floating crust can be tried in the hope that the carp have since lost the memory of its danger.

This attitude is, I believe, at the heart of successful carp fishing. For it involves being always one step ahead of the carp. Always be prepared to try something new instead of just sitting back in the hope that a bait and method so successful in the past will continue to bring success.

This is not so difficult on the new 'hungry' or comparatively unfished waters. But when it comes to the heavily fished and difficult 'big fish' waters, the carp always seem to know what it is all about!

Every once in a while a big fish is caught. Either it makes a mistake – or the man who caught it thought of something new to try. But whichever way you care to look at it, the carp are winning. They have no need to risk danger by eating our baits. There is plenty of natural food available to them or they would not be so big in the first place.

The men who fish for really big carp know all this, but it is these very same difficulties that continue to attract them. They carry on fishing in the hope that one day they will have thought of a new bait, or a new method – presented in a certain way, at the right time and place – that will bring a carp bigger than any caught before, rolling and wallowing to their net.

When, and if, that time comes they will probably still fish on and on. For by their very nature, that is the way of the true carp angler.

TACKLE

More than in any other kind of fishing, carp tackle has to be utterly reliable in every respect. It is of little use spending several weekends in pursuit of a specimen, only to lose it because of a straightened hook, or because the line breaks at a lower breaking strain than it did the week before.

Failure of hook and line is probably the cause of at least 90 per cent of lost carp. So never be concerned about stepping up the strength of these. After all, the idea is to get a carp on the bank, and there is nothing sporting about leaving a fish with a hook in its mouth, or swimming about trailing yards of line. Hooks size 6-2/0 will suffice with lines of 6-20lb b.s., according to snags and size of carp sought.

Fibreglass rods are almost indestructible, and one of 11ft length, with action right down to the corks, is about right. Fixed-spool reels are a must. The landing net can be as large as can be reasonably manoeuvred with one arm, and with mesh deep enough to engulf anything that swims. Rod-rests should allow line to run through unhindered.

METHODS

Conventional carp fishing methods are really very simple. Almost anything edible is attached to the unweighted hook and cast out.

The rod is then placed in rod-rests so that it points down the line and the bale arm of the reel is left in the open position to await a bite. This is registered by a piece of silver paper or kitchen foil placed on the line between butt-ring and reel. The reader should need no instruction on what to do when the line runs out fast!

All things being equal, carp are more prone to feed on the shallows than in deeper waters, but there can be factors that prohibit this. On heavily-fished waters, where the shallows tend to be close to the banks, sudden drops in temperature that send fish into warm, deeper water are among such instances.

Islands, sunken humps, bars and shelves are prone to harbour carp, and so are weed beds, sunken trees and the like. If these are on shallow water surrounded by deeper water, then so much the better. For the carp's feeding areas are likely to be concentrated in such places.

In general, warm, muggy conditions are conducive to carp being (and perhaps feeding) at the surface. Cooler, less-settled conditions often find them feeding at the bottom, and a sure sign that this is in progress is when carp are leaping.

There's a good bream in the net, landed by Ray Mumford under the critical gaze of Frank Johnson, the Brixton tackle dealer and an All-England finalist.

HALL
AT SEA

WINSTON HALL is a noted authority on deepsea boat fishing and confesses this to be his favourite branch of the sport, with shore fishing as a firm second favourite. Born in Margate, on the Kent coast, and educated in London, he has now settled on the Yorkshire coast at Scarborough, close to his beloved seas.

ANGLING AFLOAT

NO sooner had Dick found a parking space than a blue-jerseyed tout had his head in the car. 'Fishing, sir?', he asked.

Before I could nudge a warning, Dick had nodded. The tout beamed. 'You want the *Mary Jane*, sir. Skipper is Bill Cranmer. Best in the business, he is. Give him this ticket and tell him Old Tom sent you.'

I'd met Dick in the hotel bar the night before. He'd shown a lively interest in my rods and I had promised him a day's angling afloat. And Dick was showing his greenness already.

Every seaside town catering for anglers swarms with touts. To take one at his word is asking for a fast one to be pulled on you. For you may be certain that Old Tom is getting a cut of every fare he sends along.

Ignoring the tout, I changed into my seaboots and left my shoes in the car. Seaboots make for heavy walking, but like oilskins or coats are easiest to carry when worn – especially when you are encumbered with rods and tackle.

The *Mary Jane* was the first craft we came across. Big, roomy and announcing herself with blaring pop music from a loudhailer, she already carried some two dozen anglers. They were a mixed crowd, the majority obvious day-trippers without tackle of their own and clutching rods and reels of an inefficient 'tackle-supplied-by-the-skipper' type.

'All very well for a jolly ride out,' I told Dick, 'but what we want is a spot of serious fishing. Let's look around.'

We passed several boats, none of which took my eye. Some were gaily painted and smart, some shabby or dirty. Most had the same fault – too many passengers. However big a boat is, all size advantage is lost with crowding.

At sea, such ships bristle with rods. As a result,

Winston Hall, afloat for a day, unhooks a young codling—a hint of bigger things to follow.

lines continually become entangled, bites are lost and tempers strained. And invariably the anglers are of that type who parade the streets on their way home dangling huge bunches of sadly under-sized fish strung on cod-line through the gills.

At last a 30-footer caught my eye. Her paintwork was the worse for wear, but that could mean only that her owner-skipper was too busy with regular summer clients to spare time with a brush.

She was spotlessly clean. Her newly-washed decks showed no sign of yesterday's bait or gutting. All ropes and lines were neatly coiled, with their ends nicely back-spliced to prevent fraying.

The bulwarks were elbow high. Just right, that. They are safe without interfering with your rod-work. You can brace yourself against them when the ship rolls, and lean your rod on the gunwale without real danger of its going overboard if you take your attention off it for a snack or a smoke.

Other points that appealed to me were the tall bows and forward cuddy. There'd be shelter from wind and spray if it brewed up nasty while we were at sea. The thwarts were wide and offered comfortable seating.

A collection of big plastic bowls stowed one inside another showed that the skipper had thoughtfully provided containers for the anglers' fish. Few things are more objectionable or dangerous than the habit of allowing slimy fish to litter a deck at sea.

Against the cuddy and firmly lodged in spring clips was a line of unspectacular but workmanlike rods, each fitted with a foolproof centre-pin reel holding monofilament of useful all-round breaking-strain. Not that any of the ten anglers already in the boat would be using the skipper's outfits. Each was busily engaged tackling up his own gear—and that gear showed plainly that those anglers were experienced men who knew what they were about.

Actually, I would have been content with only half the signs of a well-run craft. When I saw that this one had 'Licensed to carry 12 persons' painted above the stern thwart, I felt I had found the perfect combination of boat and skipper. There would be room for all to move about, and room to fish, too.

I caught the skipper's attention. 'Room for a couple more?' He shot me a shrewd glance before nodding. I liked that. Obviously he weighed his fares up, preferring to avoid novices when possible. All in all, I knew we had made a happy choice.

We were barely settled aboard before Skip threw his engine into gear and nudged his boat gently away from the quay. Once outside the harbour arms, he opened up and the powerful diesel throbbed us effortlessly through flat, calm water. Ahead a flock of gulls—each bird reflected on the oily surface—waited till the very last second before taking off in flight under our cutwater.

Dick, who claimed to be an experienced freshwater angler, had done no sea fishing before, and I had persuaded him to swallow a couple of travel pills against sea-sickness. He grinned wryly at the flat surface, but I still felt he'd taken a wise precaution. Once off in a charter boat, there is little hope of getting ashore until trip time is up. And to

Here's a familiar character caught in the act! It's Charles Derrick, well-known naturalist and fly fisher, trying his hand at sea fishing on the Isle of Arran.

e stuck in a boat for hours on end while feeling queasy is nobody's idea of fun.

I'd lent him a spare medium-weight boat rod. It was just over 6ft long and of supple hollow-glass, light yet immensely strong. His reel was a multiplier more suitable for beach-casting than for boat angling.

Nevertheless, providing he pumped his fish by continually raising the rod-tip and reeling in the line-slack so gained, he would keep most of the weight off the spool. This is important, since nylon monofilament is subject to stretch. Retrieved directly on to a reel under strain, monofilament tries to contract with such power that many a spool or end plate has suffered serious damage.

Even on the hottest day ashore, it is cool at sea. Dick had smiled earlier at my heavy sweater. Now, under the light breeze of our progress, he was glad enough to climb into a spare pullover I'd slipped into my kit with him in mind.

Our skipper passed the tiller to a passenger who was obviously a regular, and hauled three wooden boxes from the cuddy.

One held fresh mackerel bait, one lugworm, the third skeined mussel. With a 'Help yourselves, gents,' he stowed them carefully out of the sun and began looking shorewards to pick up his marks. Eventually satisfied, he cut his engine and the complete silence of a calm sea fell on us.

Dick, who had already baited each of his three

Nothing strenuous here for Winston Hall as he deals with a 17oz dab.

We cannot recall any stirring prose about four men in a boat, and this type of fishing is not everyone's choice. But the rewards are great, we are told, here in Brodick Bay, Isle of Arran.

hooks with a different lure, lifted his rod to drop his paternoster overboard. I told him to wait until the anchor was down and all movement off the ship. Otherwise, I explained, he might lose his line on the cable.

But Skip overheard me and shook his head. 'It's all right, sir, we're going to drift.'

Drifting is an effective method when there is little or no wind. The craft is allowed to go wherever wind and water take it, and a lot of ground is thus covered. The great advantage lies in the fact that when she is moving with the tide, comparatively light sinkers may be used.

Like most freshwater chaps on their first saltwater

There's nothing like an occasional conger to liven a day's sport!

venture, Dick was inclined to rest his rod and rely on watching the tip as indication of a bite. He nearly had heart failure during the first few minutes as his rod kept up a continual nodding. This, of course, was due to the lead dragging the bottom as the boat moved with the tide.

'You'll do better to hold your rod,' I said. 'You'll feel a bite plainly. It's like sharp tugs. After a little practice you'll even be able to distinguish between the bites of various species.'

Soon afterwards, Dick got his first bite and struck with a vigorous jerk of his rod. Another beginner's mistake, that.

When you are boat fishing, it never pays to be smart with your reaction. Give a fish plenty of time to get a bait into his mouth before attempting to drive your hook home in his jaws.

Experience alone will teach correct timing, but as a brief guide, a lip-hooked fish has been struck too soon, and one that has swallowed the hook too late. A hook driven into a fish's palate or side jaw has been hit just about right.

Stick to this scheme and, although you may lose a lot of little fish, you won't go far wrong with the big ones.

Our skipper had certainly put us among fish that day. Soon we all had cod, whiting, mackerel and an odd thornback ray in our bowls. Then, as the tide slackened and changed, a stiffish breeze sprang up out of the sou'-east and sport dropped off.

Once more Skip showed he knew his job. Calling on us to recover our lines, he took us to flattie grounds. There, by changing our bottom rigs from paternoster to trace with small hooks, we had good sport with dabs and plaice until the setting sun warned that it was time to return.

Taking one thing with another, we'd had a good day and fully justified our care in choosing boat and skipper.

THE HALLS AT SEA

This is the time for watchfulness . . . and Winston Hall is all concentration. 'You really can't be bothered to help your wife when shark are taking,' he says.

Reintroducing Angela

... and a woman's eye view of what is essentially a masculine sport

BY JOHN INGHAM

John Ingham has been a journalist and keen angler for more than twenty years. He introduced 'The People' Angling Club, as a reader-service project, and developed its activities for more than 50,000 members. In 1966 he became Editor of 'Angler's Mail'.

ANGLING has come a long, long way since it was either ignored by the public or, worse, labelled as a sport which merely required 'a worm at one end and a fool at the other'.

The modern angler, in his multi-thousands, is well equipped and better organised than ever before. And although, by the very nature of his sport, he still obviously must prefer to be unseen and unheard, his place in leisure activities is accepted as one of strength and importance.

But in the process of growing up–surrounding himself with all the paraphernalia of big-money freshwater competitions, organised specimen hunting and sophisticated electronic underwater sea-fishing 'eyes', plus the power and wealth of the regional and national associations to which he may subscribe–Jack the angler has been in danger of appearing to be a very dull boy indeed.

Yet this is far from true, as anyone who has tried to tap the vein of rich humour which runs through the sport will testify. The deluge of amateur cartoons which descend every week upon angling periodicals, and the comic situations that so often develop to convulse the most serious of angling occasions, are born of the sport itself.

Thankfully, humour is universal–and that applies as much to angling as a whole as to any other sport. Used with care, and with respect for those who take a deep and serious interest in their leisure occupations, there is ample scope for humour in the printed world of angling.

That is why *Angela* was created and introduced to the readers of *Angler's Mail*. She presented a woman's eye view of what is essentially a masculine sport, and she quickly established a following among amused wives and girl-friends who saw themselves in her affectionate and naïve attempts to understand anglers—and her feminine desire to take over and organise their fishing trips, often with disastrous results.

Angela was, at first, accepted less quickly by anglers themselves, who were vaguely resentful about anything that was not a serious survey of their sport and, in so doing (as they themselves gradually realised), took fish and fishing far too seriously.

Within a few months, *Angela's* send-ups had become a weekly chuckle for thousands of faithful followers. But in the natural process of editorial review, and the constant need to maintain a flow of fresh ideas, she took a 'rest', as they say in show business, and awaits her chance of a comeback.

Here, then, for those who were *Angela* fans and look forward to her return—and for those who have yet to encounter her dizzy angling ways—is my personal vintage selection of her more beguiling contributions.

Angela's true identity is a closely-guarded editorial secret. Scores of women readers wrote in to say 'she' must be a man to possess such knowledge of feminine reactions. But just as many men wrote to ask for an autographed copy of her photograph, and she lost count of the annual dinners and prize presentations she was asked to attend but had to refuse.

Man or woman, true angler or merely an observer of human nature, *Angela* was the first real attempt to soften the sobriety of what is often a lonely and incommunicative sport. And here she is, doing just that . . .

The scene is Wester Ross, one of the Morefield lochs, which are set high above Strathkanaird, north of Ullapool. The isolated peaks of Stac Polly, Cul Beog and Cul Mor stand out on the skyline.

ANGELA ON READING THE WATER———

A MASTER Specimen Hunter is he who alights from his Bentley, brushes aside his fawning associate, rakes the mist-shrouded water with one fearless, probing sweep of his steely-blue eyes and, although he has never seen the water before in his life, declares in a single, clipped phrase: 'There's a $33\frac{1}{2}$ mirror under the fourth cabbage patch in the third bay to the left of the second largest clump of stinging nettles.'

That's what I mean by being able to read the water.

But before we go any further—if you have come across such a man, there is something you must do as a matter of extreme urgency: *Put him under lock and key and send for me.*

Meanwhile, I don't want you to think that I, and my All-Girls Specimen Group, have been asleep on our feet in this art of reading the water. Far from it.

In fact, we regard it as so important that we have developed a fixed routine for dealing with a strange water.

And we have become so skilled that within a comparatively short time of arriving at a new fishery, we have ascertained the following vital information:—

> *(a) Water temperature at surface, mid-depth and bottom;*
> *(b) Depth close in and farther out;*
> *(c) Approx. speed of flow (if any);*
> *(d) Surface windspeed and direction;*
> *(e) Presence of fish and identification of species;*
> *(f) Nearest 'Ladies'.*

It goes without saying that teamwork of the highest order is needed to collect so much information so quickly.

And I'm proud to say that my All-Girls Group swings into well-drilled action like those gorgeous chaps you see nipping over chasms and things with bits of howitzers at the Royal Tournament.

WATER TEMPERATURE

That's Julia's department. On arrival at the venue we choose a likely swim and throw Julia in. The number of goose-pimples per square inch of Julia,

Now where can we have seen that face before? That's right—on the old goggle-box! It's Terry Thomas, angling correspondent for 'ATV Today'.

A crowded moment on the pier for this band of North Wales anglers.

and whether or not her teeth are chattering, tell us all we need to know about how cold or warm it is.

In the process, of course, she is also ascertaining the DEPTH – all we have to do is to note how quickly she sinks and make a fair allowance for her height. The depth close-in to the bank is also revealed if she can wade up the bank or has to be pulled up screeching.

DRIFT CHECK

Desiree deals in her own quietly efficient way with ascertaining the amount of water drift or current.

To do this, she saves walnut shells at Christmas, carefully mounts a small matchstick mast and tiny sail, and launches one for each of us in the swim.

If they go round and round it's an eddy. If they sink – it's real rough, boy. And so on.

My job in the team, as well as acting as co-ordinator and Head of Data Processing, is to climb the nearest tall tree overlooking the water and peer into the depths below for signs of life and to identify them.

When my vigil is rewarded by a 'sighting' or sounds of clooping or slurping, I drop a marker buoy stealthily (you can make them easily out of old bricks to which are attached empty plastic lemons on bits of string).

The splash not only alerts the Group to the spot where the fish were last seen, but also helps to reveal the unsuspected presence of camouflaged rival male specimen-hunters.

And I must admit their excited and colourful speculations on the size of the one that just rolled over make most interesting chapters in our reading of the water.

ANGELA AND THE FUR AND FEATHER MATCH————

AREN'T anglers a touchy lot? Just because of one or two trivial happenings – for which I got the

blame—at that Christmas Fur and Feather match they talked me into, everyone's been telling me off. Warning me off, even. It just isn't fair.

Well, if they were so keen to have a girl at their silly little match why didn't they organise the thing properly? We squashed into the coach—and I do mean squashed, though don't think me a spoilsport—and stopped at every pub in sight.

The pints of beer they sank. Fantastic! 'It's Christmas, ducks,' they kept saying — pushing another stout into my hand.

When we did reach the river, simply hours later, all the fellers just flew out of the coach and headed for the woods with strangely joyous cries. I ran after them like mad, thinking it was a race for the best swims. But when they saw me coming, they broke cover like startled partridges. And they all turned their backs on me! Wasn't that unfriendly—just before Christmas, too?

Then, look at their grouchy behaviour over what happened just before we went home. They blew a whistle and said that was that, everybody out and because I hadn't caught anything, they said I could be the one who put the fish back at the way in after they'd had a coffee at the coach.

Well, I couldn't find the way in, any more than I could find the way out. But I did come across several peculiarly-shaped nets suspended in the water with lots of poor fish trapped inside. So I did my good deed for the day and released them and hurried over to the coach with the news.

John Goddard's deepsea chums are seen endeavouring to boat a large tunny during the trip described in Page 40. Below, the matchbox by the mouth gives some indication of the size of the eye of the big-eyed tunny.

Do you know, they seemed quite overcome, almost demented! One boy I rather fancied–it was the pompom on his hat (rather dashing)–actually threw himself on the ground beating the grass with his fists! What a carry on! His broken cries made me realise he was worrying about those fish. So I reassured him gently that none of the fish–fourteen 'goers', I think he called them–was bleeding when I let them go.

The chaps didn't speak to me all the way home. Even when I asked who won. But you can't tell with men, can you? They go all silent like that, without a word of warning.

Back to my angling lessons next week–and if you're thinking of running a fur and feather match next Christmas, I shall be happy to do my fish rescues again.

ANGELA'S TACKLE BAG———

I THINK it was very noble of Frank Guttfield to lift the lid on his tackle secrets. After all, it's not every Specimen Hunter who would throw open his tackle bag like a Stately Home and let us have a look around inside, is it?

My tackle bag is an all-purpose affair, carefully designed to cope with all eventualities likely to be foreseen in any fishing trip–and every man for himself otherwise.

Though I don't have Frank's skill at taking pictures, I can give you a good idea of the useful size of my tackle bag by mentioning that, in addition to all the angling essentials, it will also hold 7lb of potatoes, 2lb of Spring greens, 1lb small onions and some nice young carrots on a Saturday, when I'm throwing together one of my fabulous Irish stews.

As for the contents, I can best help newcomers to specimen hunting by turning out my bag and listing the contents–all of which, I do assure you, cannot be done without.

1) *Little black dress*, in case I'm invited out to dinner during the match. Well, you never know your luck in some of these big Open events.

2) *Shoes* to go with little black dress. I do feel it is asking for unfortunate misunderstandings to turn

Season of new hope..

. . . for the salmon fishers on the River Eden, seen here on a crisp January morning at Armathwaite, Cumberland.

All neatly 'parcelled' in the line, a conger is lifted still wriggling to the rocks.

up in Wellington boots, and they're so inhibiting if you try to dance in them.

3) *Two extra sweaters* in case the sun goes in.

4) *Bikini* in case the sun comes out.

5) *Emergency battle kit* of lipsticks, eye-liners, spare eyelashes, eyebrow pencils, nail varnishes, etc.—all the usuals.

6) *First-aid kit*—an absolute essential as I may be called to the scene at any time and, as a woman, they will naturally turn to me with trust and faith in their pain-filled eyes. So I always carry a nurse's white cap, a pretty frilly starched apron, a pen-knife (for emergency ops), vodka (for anaesthetic) and an aspirin.

7) *Emergency food pack* in case he decides to take out the punt again. He's an absolute fool with that punt, and I'm getting sick and tired of that little island and the bush I have to grab at if we aren't to go over the weir like a scene from 'African Queen'. (But I don't know, though, I rather fancied Mr Allnutt.)

8) *Disaster pack* comprising small gold safety pins, a penny and bus fare home.

9) *A bent float* (I sat on it).

10) *A hook*.

There now. That just about covers my Specimen Hunting outfit. If it doesn't quite contain all the items you wish, just do as I do and borrow from the others.

What's the point of a girl humping all those rods and things when all the men take at least two rods too many and can only fish properly with one at a time?

ANGELA'S CITATION———

I'M SO THRILLED, I really am! Do you know what—I've had a citation from one of the clubs I sometimes go out with. Isn't it wonderful?

I simply must let you read the whole thing just as it came through the post, all done up in parchment and fancy writing. This is what it says:

TO ANGELA—A CITATION

We her fellow-members, meeting behind locked doors above the Public Bar, wish to place on record the following significant contributions made by

Fly fishing on the Stour, where a 'fuzzy' artificial, or a moth, could take a big chub.

Angela towards Club Harmony and Fraternal Spirit in the past season.

1) BY ASSISTING as map-reader for the relief driver of the coach on the occasion of our Club Championship, she did achieve for us an additional eighty miles Mystery Tour of the countryside before reaching our venue, thus shortening the match by more than half.

2) BY ASSISTING the Scalesman upon the occasion of our Challenge Shield semi-final, she did generously adjust the achievements of all who weighed-in by recording Drams in the Ounces column and occasionally vice-versa, thus affording us the unique opportunity of fishing the match all over again.

3) BY FALLING in the river upon the occasion of the President's Match, she did afford us the opportunity of vacating our swims while she changed into OUR dry clothing behind the bushes. We also wish to

place on record that the Club, who loaned us the fishery for the day, has afforded us the unexpected opportunity of selecting another fishery next year due to our explanations not being accepted as to the reasons for a bra and frilly panties and other feminine garments being suspended from their 'Private Fishing' notice board when their Bailiff came around.

4) BY HER PROMPT ACTION in waving a red scarf at Farmer Brown's bull when it inadvertently strayed into the bottom meadow of our fishery during a New Year Match, she afforded all who were physically capable the opportunity of keeping warm with a brisk race to the fence. She also showed great presence of mind in making an emergency stretcher for our Chairman, who badly misjudged the height of the fence. We wish to assure *Angela*

that her skill at making a stretcher out of pieces of Farmer Brown's fence has not gone unnoticed by Farmer Brown.

5) IN RECOGNITION of the above-mentioned contributions, we wish *Angela* to know that a Collection is being taken up among ourselves to provide her with a Free Pass to the Odeon, valid on Saturdays and Sundays.

Signed (in blood) by all members.

There! Aren't they truly wonderful boys? I'm so fond of them all. But, bless the silly darlings, they've forgotten I shall be going fishing with them at weekends and couldn't go to the pictures as well.

Don't worry, I'll just say nothing and turn up as usual. Between you and me, they need my feminine influence to look after them on their fishing trips.

All aboard Dennis, *the Flamborough coble, as it is manhandled afloat.*

FREE-LINE
FUN
FISHING

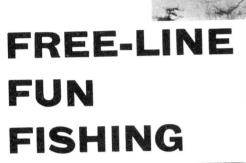

● *JOHN PIPER, a big name in angling journalism, loves to roam around British and Irish rivers and streams lightly equipped with a single rod and, usually, a tin of lobworms.*

● *THIS is his favourite fishing—free-lining with 'lobs' in a way that is completely different from the static methods employed by float-fishing enthusiasts and the ranks of match-men.*

BY

JOHN

PIPER

I HAVE no idea who invented free-line angling. A native of New Guinea, perhaps, or an Ancient Briton returning to the comfort of Cheddar Caves. Whoever it was, he had the right idea. For it is a simple method, involving less tackle than any other, and is often ideal for the roving angler. What's more, it's great fun!

No float is used. No $\frac{1}{4}$oz lead shatters the surface to plummet worm or flake to the riverbed. The bait provides its own casting weight and falls as it might from a tree or bank, to be carried by the current and to sink slowly, naturally, to the fish below.

Free-lining can be passive or active, as you wish. My own preference is for a light rod and water so clear that I can track upstream, casting to chub or trout, roach or grayling spotted from cover on the bankside.

This is no sport for the angler who is loaded with stool and keepnet, tackle box, holdall and groundbait. A rod, landing net and haversack must suffice. Sometimes a single rod-rest is useful and, always, a pair of Polaroid sunglasses. Nothing more. Let others tote everything but the kitchen sink: the free-liner travels light.

But if you have never fished this way, one question has yet to be answered. With no float, no leger rig, how can one tell when a fish takes the bait?

On the crystal waters of the Hampshire Avon, and its tributaries, you will often actually SEE the fish take, certainly during the summer months. The same must apply to the chalk streams of the North and to some of Ireland's delightful fisheries. But there are very few waters where you can see the bottom all the time.

A breeze ruffles the surface more often than not. Many carrier streams and backwaters are dark and weeded, with little or no current at the height of the summer. But here, too, is a situation tailor-made for free-lining.

You may use bread-flake in large chunks, bunched brandlings, dead minnow for chub in the early months of the season, bread paste, cheese and various natural baits. But the finest all-rounder is the lobworm. Tough and active, it is irresistible to most species, easily found, easily kept in tip-top condition and heavy enough to cast more yards than you are ever likely to need.

So let's cast a lob and, with a flick of the rod, send our choicest worm and its size 8 hook across the water to the very edge of that lily bed. (*Sometimes*

A 3½lb Avon trout, taken by John Piper using his favourite free-line techniques.

110

Free-line fishing: Tighten line to form a slight bow between surface and rod-tip. As the bait is taken the line will tighten, as indicated by the dotted line in the sketch. And that is when you strike!

we'll take a chance and deliberately cast into the very midst of the lilies.)

Worm and surface meet with a 'plop'. The lob sinks, grey-white and wriggling, until it disappears from sight. Our 4lb line settles on the surface, then follows the bait down as the rod is held . . . waiting.

Don't pay too much attention to the water rats moving on the far side, or to the sparrowhawk hovering above the next field. Wait and watch, that's the rule. Many a chub and no small number of trout have taken the bait at this moment. So, too, have pike and perch, and they have taken without hesitation.

The line runs tight; a lift of the rod-tip and the fish is on. A leger lead or a float heavy enough to cover the same distance could have scared the living daylights out of them, and sent those fish darting upstream or diving to the nearest shelter. But not the free-line worm!

On this occasion, nothing happens. Give the bait time to settle, then gently – very gently – recover the slack line. And as the nylon begins to tighten move the reel handle a mere half-turn in reverse. The line drops to form a slight bow between rod-tip and surface – and there's your bite indicator, gleaming like a monorail in the morning sun. When that line twitches, straightens and starts to cut the surface like a cheese wire . . . STRIKE!

One hears a lot about shy-biting tench on some waters, fish that only twitch the bait and then, apparently, drop it. It seems to me that a hungry fish reacts this way only if suspicious of the bait or of resistance set up by float or leads.

If you encounter such fish, strip off your float and fish free-line with lobs or brandlings or flake. You may be pleasantly surprised at the result. And don't leave that bait too long in one place. An occasional twitch from your end can persuade a cruising tench that if he doesn't act soon, a likely source of food will escape.

The same killing technique can be employed in weirpools and undercut swims favoured by chub and perch, although the line reacts very differently to that poised above still-water. It will obviously pull tight as the bait is swept away in the turbulent waters of a weirpool, only to fall slack as the same currents change course and sweep the bait back towards the rod.

Let it roam as it will. Watch the rod-top for signs

of action. There is no mistaking the knock as a fish makes off with the bait.

Don't worry if your rod is of a different design to mine or to that carried by the first man you meet on the water. If it has a fairly delicate top and you can carry it happily for the best part of the day, it will do.

I've been fishing this way, on and off, for many years and I've accumulated a stock of rods much as a keen golfer collects clubs–more than he ever needs for any one game.

Two dainty built-cane rods, 7ft and 8ft long, both capable of throwing a fly line but with handles fitted for fixed spool operations, are my favourite weapons. A tougher, 10ft model in fibreglass serves wherever snags or pike (or both) are known features of the underwater scene.

The months pass all too quickly, and in winter a variation of the free-line worm offers a splendid alternative to trotting the stream. The waving, trailing green weed of summertime has all but disappeared and the bait moves almost unhindered

All is still, as an angler worm-fishes for sea trout on a North Country river.

'X' marks the angler in action, casting part-way across the river on his first cast (A). His second cast (B) should reach across the water. Each cast is fished in a wide arc before moving downstream to repeat the operation with casts C and D.

through the water. A swan shot, nipped on to the line a foot above the hook, will be needed to sink the bait, and you may even prefer to hold the line in your left hand and feel for the bites.

Much depends on local conditions, and I readily admit that at this stage our free-line tackle comes close to being a fixed leger.

Cast up and only part-way across, letting the current carry the bait in an arc until it lies directly below you, downstream. Retrieve and cast again, but this time cast as far across-river as you can. No reaction? Move down a few paces and start again.

It is great exercise; it covers a lot of water, and when the fish are feeding there is excitement that only a fly fisherman or spinner can match.

In deep holes use the free-line worm, singly or bunched to form an 'octopus', or put a dead minnow on the hook and fish either bait sink-and-

draw. When the perch are tight-shoaled, waiting for the spring before dispersing to stations along the river, sport can be of the stuff that dreams are made of.

Lead on the line? Only you can judge the water, but generally speaking the less lead the better, and no lead is best of all.

When winter's frosts are on the ground, or a keen wind is blowing, it is more fun to be active and to hunt your fish in this way. To me, certainly, it is a great deal warmer than huddling over a static float or a leger rod that may be frozen to the rod-rests!

The Scots rise early—and here's a before-breakfast sea trout from the River Annan.

If you catch a record fish...

BY PETER TOMBLESON

PETER TOMBLESON, F.Z.S., is secretary of the National Anglers' Council and the British Record (rod-caught) Fish Committee. Here he describes what you, the angler, must do if you wish to claim a new record ... and what the Committee will do in assessing the validity of your claim.

DEEP in the heart of most anglers, whether they are freshwater or sea fishermen, is a desire to catch a big fish. For some anglers this is the spur which drives them on to experiment with tackle and techniques and to roam far afield in search of new waters. The match angler, usually well content to catch plenty of fish rather than a few large ones, welcomes bigger fish when they come along.

For the majority of anglers the record fish never comes along; the chances of catching one are fairly remote, but they are not so remote that it is out of the question. Few record fish are caught deliberately, a fact that should encourage the merest novice.

Some anglers, using great technical skill and exploiting their own wide knowledge of the species and its location, have planned to catch record fish and have been successful. Their stories, which sometimes have spanned a period of years of real dedication, have served to encourage others whose ambition is to catch the largest fish of a particular species. What should serve to encourage them further is the accepted fact that, in the sea and in fresh water, there are still plenty of record-breaking fish to be caught.

The British Record (Rod-Caught) Fish Committee, established in 1957, investigates and adjudicates all record claims for fish caught in the United Kingdom, including Northern Ireland and the Channel Islands. Over the years the Committee has investigated more than one hundred claims for record fish, the majority being sea fish. A large number of these claims have been substantiated and accepted as new British records.

What sort of procedure is involved and how does it work?

The Committee is a completely independent body, working under the auspices of the National Anglers' Council, the responsible body for angling in England and Wales. It meets regularly three times a year to consider claims, and its aims and objects are fairly simple: it investigates and approves or rejects record claims, maintains a file of this information and publishes a record list every year.

It has the co-operation of the majority of anglers who recognise it as the official record fish body, and it has the support of various other organisations, such as local Area Specimen Fish Panels, the universities, the British Museum and the Marine Biological Association, to help it overcome the most important problem involved in making claims – the correct identification of the fish. The Bailiwick of Guernsey Record (Rod-Caught) Fish Committee and the Jersey Specimen and Records (Rod-Caught) Fish Committee assist with claims from the Channel Islands.

When an angler catches a fish which he thinks is a record, he should immediately contact the

It's the big one in the net, home and dry, that counts when record hunting – like the nice double-figure capture in this picture. But record claims don't end here, as Peter Tombleson explains.

When you're pulling a big 'un into the boat, or fishing a shoreline nearer home,
it's vital to know the record claim procedure, says Tombleson.

secretary of the Committee, while still retaining the fish either alive or preserved in a deep freeze—or in a liquid preservative such as formalin.

The secretary will then advise on how the fish should be identified. This is usually done by having the body sent to the Department of Zoology, Liverpool University, which carries out most of the identification work, or to the British Museum or the Marine Biological Association if the fish is a sea fish.

Once the fish is correctly identified, the claimant receives a set of forms to be filled in. These require the signatures of witnesses to the capture and to the weighing of the fish. In addition, a certificate from a local Weights and Measures Inspector must be produced to verify that the scales used for the weighing of the fish were accurate.

If the angler was fishing alone, then he must be prepared to swear before a Commissioner for Oaths that he caught the fish by fair angling. Foulhooked fish and fish whose weight may be enhanced by disease are not eligible for claims.

The Committee may also require photographs of the fish to be produced. In certain circumstances the body of the fish may not be required, but certainly in that event the claimant must produce acceptable photographs. These must show the fish clearly, its fin shapes and their position.

The Committee sets a high standard. It must be satisfied beyond reasonable doubt that the claim is in order. If all the requirements are met then the claim goes forward to the Committee.

Serving on this are scientists and anglers who sit

You're never too young to catch a record-buster, but is it necessary to risk life and limb?

Rays are difficult to identify, but the spots on the wings of this Cuckoo ray are clearly distinguishable. This record five-pounder came from off the Isle of Arran.

and give impartial judgment on all claims. Their main interest is whether the fish was caught fairly and was witnessed, identified and weighed correctly. All being in order the fish will be accepted and the captor issued with a certificate to show that, at the date given, he caught the largest fish of that species.

This is the standard procedure. But problems do often occur. Some anglers, especially freshwater enthusiasts, catch a large fish for which they wish to claim a record yet they wish to return the fish to the water. This is understandable and the Committee accepts this point. In such cases the angler must keep the fish alive until it is seen by someone appointed by the Committee to identify and weigh it or witness the weighing. Provided this happens, the fish may then be returned.

Anglers may catch record fish and have no facilities for keeping the body preserved for inspec-

RECORDS . . . *come in several shapes and sizes, and claims are now awaited for various species. Such as the Crucian carp (left), pike (above) and chub (netted below). Sadly, none of these makes the minimum qualifying weight laid down.*

tion. In such cases the Committee usually advises that space in a deep freeze is obtainable for the necessary period. Often a local butcher or fishmonger will help.

If the fish is quite small, it can be kept for long periods in a solution of formalin (obtainable from any chemist) mixed with water: one tablespoon of formalin – 40 per cent solution of formaldehyde – to a pint of water.

There are other problems. Sometimes, a fish weighed at the waterside is found to have lost weight when it is put on the scales later. Which weight goes on the claim form?

The answer is that the weight for which the fish is claimed must be properly witnessed and authenticated. If this can be done immediately after capture, then this is the weight to be shown on the claim forms. If it cannot be weighed and witnessed until some time later, then the later weight is put down.

Speed in having a newly-caught fish weighed and witnessed is essential because fish certainly lose weight after capture, even when they are kept in water.

Anglers also ask if a fish in spawn should be counted – referring to large female pike which are in spawn in winter and heavier than they would be earlier or later in the year. The answer is that spawn in a fish is a natural part of the body.

A predatory fish may also have just eaten another fish and will be slightly heavier than when its stomach is empty. This, too, is quite natural and is part of the weight of the fish.

But there have been other instances of fish with abnormal weights due to dropsy, which adds water to the body, and this is not a natural condition. Occasionally a fish may be in a spawn-bound condition with an abnormal weight due to excessive eggs which have not been shed or re-absorbed. Again this is an unnatural condition.

Problems of identification are the great concern of the Committee for, despite the common occurrence of some fish, these still cannot be easily identified by anglers. Chub are commonly mistaken for roach; rudd for roach; bronze or common bream for silver bream. There are also cyprinid hybrids such as roach-bream, rudd-bream and roach-rudd which are difficult for the average angler to identify.

Only an expert can help, hence the rule that requires the body of the fish to be retained until instructions dealing with its identification are received from the secretary.

Among the sea fishes there are more problems of identification because there are more species involved. Bull huss (greater-spotted dogfish) are often thought to be lesser-spotted dogfish. The wrasses are difficult to distinguish, and the skates and rays also present problems.

In freshwater fish, anglers often mislead themselves by thinking that coloration is an important guide to identification. It is probably the least reliable guide, yet in sea fish the colour of the under-surface of skates and rays is important.

The expert uses many characteristics to identify fish, including the location of fins, the number of fin rays – soft and spiny – the teeth, the eyes, the back-

Unhooking a Blagdon brownie of 1lb 10oz.

121

bone, the scales and the gill covers. In certain rays the size, shape and location of the ocelli (large spots) is important, and without a key to guide him on these the layman may often make a mistake.

Even professional boatmen, who usually have a wide knowledge of fish, can slip up occasionally in the identification of some sea fish. In gurnards, for example, the swim bladder may need to be examined.

But the Record Committee accepts that the angler is not a biologist and its rules allow for this. It has available experts on fish who can identify the species accurately, but they will almost certainly not do so unless they can examine the body.

Occasionally the Committee is criticised for accepting on to its list fairly rare fish and quite small fish. It is important to realise that the Committee is not in the least concerned with the ethics of which species of fish anglers should catch. The Committee's job is to record for posterity the capture by fair angling of the largest fish of any species that comes along.

Its job is to investigate and record, and this it does to the utmost of its ability.

Not a sound . . . not a ripple . . . and probably not the slightest thought about record-breaking!

BRITISH RECORD FISH LIST

IN DECEMBER, 1968, the meeting of the British Record (rod-caught) Fish Committee of the National Anglers' Council revised the long-standing list of records. As a result of this revision, twelve freshwater and two sea record fish were dropped from the list, and minimum qualifying weights were announced for the vacancies thus created. The record list printed below, including the vacant records, is correct at time of going to press.

Freshwater Fish

FISH	WEIGHT	CAPTOR	WHERE CAUGHT	YEAR
	lb. oz. dms.			
Bleak	0 3 8	N. D. Sizmur	Walton, Surrey	1963
*Carp	44 0 0	R. Walker	Redmire Pool	1952
Catfish	33 12 0	R. A. P. Hutt	Claydon Park	1961
Eel	7 8 0	Bob Jones	Greystone Lake	1968
Gwyniad	1 4 0	J. R. Williams	Llyn Tegid	1965
Pike-Perch (Walleye)	11 12 0	F. Adams	Welney	1934
Pike-Perch (European)	10 4 0	R. A. Watcham	Gt. Ouse Relief Channel	1968
*Roach	3 14 0	W. Penney	Lambeth Res.,	1938
	3 14 0	A. Brown	Stamford	1964
*Rudd	4 8 0	Rev. E. C. Alston	Thetford	1933
Ruffe	0 3 13	T. Gunton	River Thurne	1967
*Salmon	64 0 0	Miss G. W. Ballantyne	River Tay	1922
Tench	9 1 0	J. Salisbury	Hemingford Grey,	1963
Trout, Brown	18 2 0	K. J. Grant	Loch Garry	1965
*Trout, Rainbow	8 8 0	Lt.-Col. Creagh-Scott	Blagdon	1924

Denotes fish for which the cast or body is available for inspection. Caught before the formation of the Committee.

SPECIES OPEN FOR CLAIMS
(with minimum qualifying weights)

Barbel	13lb	Dace	1lb 4oz	Pike 41lb
Chub	7lb 8oz	Grayling	4lb	Sea trout 20lb
Common bream ..	11lb	Gudgeon	3oz 8dm	Silver bream .. 2lb
Crucian carp ..	3lb 8oz	Perch	4lb 8oz	

NOTE: The above qualifying weights are subject to revision by the Committee if necessary.

Sea Fish

FISH	WEIGHT			CAPTOR	WHERE CAUGHT	YEAR
	lb.	oz.	dms.			
Allis Shad	3	4	8	B. H. Stone	Torquay	1964
Angler Fish	68	2	0	H. G. T. Legerton	Canvey Island,	1967
Bass	18	2	0	F. C. Borley	Felixstowe	1943
Blonde Ray	32	11	0	B. R. Crabb	Skerries	1967
Bogue	1	9	14	Mrs S. O'Brien	Sorel Point,	1968
Brill	16	0	0	A. H. Fisher	Isle of Man	1950
Bull Huss	21	3	0	J. Holmes	Looe	1955
Coalfish	23	8	0	H. Millais	Land's End	1921
Common Topknot	0	6	14	R. K. Payne	Guernsey	1968
Conger	84	0	0	H. A. Kelly	Dungeness	1933
Cod	44	8	0	B. Jones	Barry	1966
Cuckoo Ray	5	0	0	N. C. McLean	Lamlash Bay,	1968
Cuckoo Wrasse	1	3	10	P. Ozouf	Guernsey	1968
Dab	2	10	12	A. B. Hare	Skerries	1968
Flounder	5	11	8	A. G. L. Cobbledick	Fowey	1956
Garfish	2	9	2	A. W. Bodfield	Dartmouth	1963
Greater Weever	2	4	0	P. Ainslie	Brighton	1927
Gurnard	11	7	4	C. W. King	Wallasey	1952
Haddock	8	12	0	Mrs Jean Graney	Whitby	1967
Hake	25	5	8	H. W. Steele	Belfast Lough	1962
Halibut	161	12	0	W. E. Knight	Marwick Head,	1968
John Dory	10	12	0	B. L. Perry	Porthallow,	1963
Lesser Spotted Dogfish	3	12	8	A. Gibson	Firth of Clyde	1967
Dogfish, spur	16	12	8	R. Legge	Chesil Beach	1964
Ling	45	0	0	H. C. Nicholl	Penzance	1912
Lumpsucker	6	3	4	F. Harrison	Redcar	1968
Mackerel	4	11	0	L. A. Seward	Flamborough Head	1963
Megrim	3	10	0	D. DiCicco	Ullapool	1966
Monkfish	66	0	0	C. G. Chalk	Shoreham	1965
Mullet, Grey	10	1	0	P. C. Libby	Portland	1952
Mullet, Red	3	10	0	J. E. Martel	Guernsey	1967
Plaice	7	15	0	I. B. Brodie	Salcombe	1964

FISH	WEIGHT			CAPTOR	WHERE CAUGHT	YEAR
	lb.	oz.	dms.			
Pollack	23	8	0	G. Bartholomew	Newquay	1957
Poor Cod	0	5	8	F. Kelly	Gourock	1967
	0	5	8	J. D. Chisholm	Berwickshire	1968
Pouting	4	10	0	H. B. Dare	Coverack	1935
Ray's Bream	7	15	12	Master G. Walker	Crimdon Beach,	1967
Red Bream	7	8	0	A. F. Bell	Fowey	1925
Red Gurnard	3	1	0	J. Tooth	Skerries Bank	1967
Scad	3	3	0	J. B. Thornton	Deal	1934
Shark, Blue	218	0	0	N. Sutcliffe	Looe	1959
Shark, Thresher	280	0	0	H. A. Kelly	Dungeness	1933
Shark, Mako	498	8	0	K. Burgess	Looe	1966
Shark, Porbeagle	324	0	0	T. Prince	Nab Tower	1968
Skate, Common	214	0	0	J. A. E. Olsson	Scapa Flow	1968
Small-Eyed Ray	10	14	4	P. Eaton	Perranporth	1968
Spotted Ray	5	8	0	M. Waterston	Luce Bay,	1968
Sting Ray	59	0	0	J. M. Buckley	Clacton	1952
Undulate Ray	10	10	4	G. Robert	Guernsey	1968
Thornback Ray	38	0	0	J. Patterson	Rustington	1935
Smooth Hound	6	3	0	W. D. J. Runnalls	Trevose Head,	1968
Sole	4	1	14	R. A. Austin	Guernsey	1967
Tope	74	11	0	A. B. Harries	Caldy Island	1964
Torsk	12	1	0	D. Pottinger	Bressay, Shetland	1968
Tunny	851	0	0	L. Mitchell Henry	Whitby	1933
Three-Bearded Rockling	2	13	2	K. Westaway	Portland Harbour	1966
Five-Bearded Rockling	0	9	4	P. R. Winder	Lancing	1968
Turbot	29	0	0	G. M. W. Garnsey	The Manacles	1964
Twaite Shad	3	2	0	T. Hayward	Deal	1949
	3	2	0	S. Jenkins	Torbay	1954
Whiting	6	0	0	E. H. Tame	Loch Shieldaig	1940
Witch	1	2	13	T. J. Barathy	Colwyn Bay	1967

SPECIES OPEN FOR CLAIMS

(with minimum qualifying weights)

Ballan wrasse   ..   6lb   Black bream   ..   3lb 8oz

NOTE: The above qualifying weights are subject to revision by the Committee, if necessary.

● **COPIES of the record fish list, rules and claim forms may be obtained from the secretary, Mr P. H. Tombleson, National Anglers' Council, Peakirk, Peterborough (Glinton 428) or from Fishmongers' Hall, London, E.C.4 (01-626 8591).**

YOUR A-to-Z RIVER GUIDE

Controlling River Authorities, Fishery Officers and Licences

AVON AND DORSET: Hampshire Avon, Stour, Frome, Piddle, Brit and Char (rivers joining sea Lyme Regis to Christchurch). S, s. £5, w. £2, d. £1; T, s. 30/-, w. 6/-; FF, s. 5/-, under 14 no charge. J. D. Brayshaw, Rostherne, 3, St. Stephen's Road, Bournemouth (Tel. Bournemouth 24708/9).

BRISTOL AVON: Avon (Bristol) and tributaries, incl. Bristol Frome, Chew, Boyd, By-Brook, Midford Brook, Cam Brook, Wellow Brook, Somerset Frome, Biss, Semington Brook, Marden, Brinkworth Brook, Kennet and Avon Canal (Bath–Devizes), Barrow No. 3, Chew Magna, Chew Valley, Litton Upper and Lower Reservoirs of Bristol Waterworks. T, s. 10/-, w. 4/-, FF, 5/- p.a., w. 2/-, under 16, 6d. p.a., from tackle dealers, club secretaries. Mr. E. E. Tucker, Green Park Road, Bath (Tel. Bath 24275/6).

CORNWALL: Tamar, Tavy, Plym, Yealm, and tributaries; Fowey and tributaries; Camel and Allen and tributaries. S, MT and T; s. £3, w. £1 10/-, d. 10/-; T, s. 15/-, w. 7/6d., d. 2/-. N. P. Cummins, St. Johns, Western Road, Launceston, Cornwall (Tel. Launceston 2151).

CUMBERLAND: Annas, Esk, Mite, Irt, Bleng, Calder, Ehen, Keekle, Marron, Derwent, Cocker, Greta, Ellen Waver, Wampool, Eden, Caldew, Petteril, Eamont, Leith, Lyvennet, Lowther, Irthing, Esk (Border), Liddle, Lyne, and tributaries; Lakes Wastwater, Ennerdale Water, Loweswater, Crummock Water, Buttermere. S, s. for whole area, £10 10/-, 7 d. £4. T (incl. MT, C), s. for whole area except S.W. Cumberland, £2. Border Esk district (south of Border only): S, s. £5, 7 d. £1 15/-, d. 10/-; T (incl. MT, C), s. £1 (under 14, 5/-), 7 d. 7/6d., d. 2/6d. EDEN DISTRICT: S, s. £7 (whole district), £4 (Eden upstream of Armathwaite Weir), £3 (Eden upstream of Temple Sowerby Bridge), £4 (Eden downstream of N.E. fence, field No. 595 in 2nd ed. O.S. of Linstock). 7 d. £2 10/-, d. 15/-; T (incl. MT, C), s. £1 (juv. under 14, 5/-), 7 d. 7/6d., d. 2/6d. Ellen and Allnoby Bay District; S, s. £1; T (incl. MT, C.), s. 10/- (under 14, 5/-), 7 d. 5/-. Derwent district: S, s. £5 (whole district), £4 (Derwent only downstream of Ouse Bridge), £2 (Derwent and tributaries, lakes upstream of Ouse Bridge and Cocker, tributaries and lakes above Waterloo Bridge, Cockermouth), £1 10/- (Cocker only upstream Waterloo Bridge), £1 10/- (Derwent, tributaries and lakes upstream of Ouse Bridge), 7 d. £1; T (incl. MT, C), s. £1 (juv. under 14 5/3d., excl. MT), 7 d. 7/6d., d. 2/6d. S.W. Cumberland: S and/or MT, s. £2 10/- (under 16, 10/-), 7 d. £1; T (excl. MT) and C, s. £1, 7 d. 7/6d. Norman Mackenzie, London Road, Carlisle, Cumberland (Tel. Carlisle 25151/2).

DEVON: Avon (Devon), Erme, Axe, Dart, Exe, Taw, Torridge, Teign and tributaries, East and West Lyn, Otter, Sid. S and T, s. £6 (whole area); for any one of Dart, Exe, Taw, Torridge or Teign and its tributaries, s. £4, w. £1 10/-, d. 7/6d.; for any one of Axe, Lyn, Heddon, Avon, Erme, Sid and Otter, s. £2, w. 10/-, d. 5/-; under 16,

s. 15/- for whole area; under 16, for any one river and its tributaries, s. 10/-, w. 2/6d. MT only, s. £1 10/- (whole area); for any one river and its tributaries, s. £1, w. 5/-, d. 2/6d. F. J. Nott, County Hall, Exeter (Tel. Exeter 77977).

GREAT OUSE: Great Ouse (incl. Relief Channel, Denver Sluice to beyond Saddle Bow Bridge), Cam and tributaries. T and FF, s. 5/- p.a.; d. 1/6d. C. H. Fennell, Elmhurst, Brooklands Avenue, Cambridge (Tel. Camb. 61561).

KENT: Medway, Stour, Rother, Darent, Cray, Royal Military Canal and tributaries; all other waters in the Board's area. T, s. 7/6d.; FF, s. 3/-; T and FF, d. (and junior season) 1/-. M. Gibson, Kent River Authority, College Avenue, Maidstone, Kent (Tel. Maidstone 55211).

EAST SUFFOLK AND NORFOLK: Bure, Yare, Waveney, Blythe, Deben, Gipping, Glaven, Stiffkey and tributaries, all other rivers and tributaries, all lakes and other waters in Norfolk and Suffolk between but excl. Heacham River in the north-west to and incl. River Gipping and its estuary, the Orwell, in the south-east. MT, 10/- p.a.; T, 10/- p.a.; FF, 5/- p.a., d. 1/-. Fisheries Officer: East Suffolk and Norfolk River Authority, The Cedars, 14 Albemarle Road, Norwich (Tel. Norwich 53257/8).

HAMPSHIRE: Test, Itchen, Hamble, Meon, Beaulieu, Lymington, Fletch, Keyhaven and tributaries. S (on Hambel, Meon, Beaulieu, Lymington, Fletch, Keyhaven and tributaries), s. £1 10/-, m. £1, w. 10/-, d. 3/6d.; elsewhere, s. £3, m. £2, w. £1, d. 7/6d.; T, s. 15/-, m. 7/6d., w. 3/6d. G. A. Wheatley, The Castle, Winchester, Hampshire (Tel. Winchester 4411).

LANCASHIRE: Ribble, Wyre, Lune, Keer, Bela, Kent, Winster, Leven, Crake, Duddon and tributaries; Lakes Windermere, Coniston, Grasmere, Rydal Water, Elterwater, etc. S, s. £5 (whole area), £4 (northern rivers only), w. £1; estuaries of Duddon, Leven, Crake and Kent, s. £2 10/-; Lune, s. £4, w. £1; Rawthey and Upper Lune, s. £2 10/-; Wyre and Keer, s. £1 10/-; Ribble, s. £2 10/-, w. 15/-; MT (whole area), s. £1 15/-, w. 15/-; NT (whole area), s. 15/-, w. 5/-; FF (whole area), s. 5/-, under 16 at reduced rates. L. Stewart, 5, St. Nicholas Street, Lancaster (Tel. Lancaster 54921).

ESSEX: Stour, Colne, Blackwater, Chelmer, Crouch, Roding and tributaries; all other streams in Essex except Lee, Stort and their tributaries. S, MT, NT, 10/-; FF, 4/-. H. Fish, Rivers House, Springfield Road, Chelmsford, Essex (Tel. Chelmsford 57281).

ISLE OF WIGHT: Eastern, Yar, Medina, Shalfleet Brook (Caul Bourne) and tributaries. Coarse fishing, 5/- (year or part), T, 10/6d. R. H. Adams, Car Park Building, County Hall, Newport, Isle of Wight (Tel. Newport, Wight, 2039).

LEE: Lee and its tributaries Licences: nil. R. G. Toms, The Grange Crossbrook Street, Cheshunt, Herts (Tel. Waltham Cross 27881).

LINCOLNSHIRE: Witham and tributaries, incl. Slea, Bain, Steeping River, Ancholme, South Forty Foot Drain, Hobhole Drain, East and West Fen Drains, etc. T, 10/- p.a., 7 d. 3/-; FF, 5/- p.a., 7 d. 1/6d. G. A. Farrow, 50, Wide Bargate, Boston, Lincs (Tel. Boston 3921/2/3).

MERSEY AND WEAVER: Mersey, Irwell, Alt, Bollin, Weaver, Dane, Gowy, and tributaries. No fishery byelaws or licence duties at time of going to press. R. E. Woodwards, Liverpool Road, Great Sankey, Warrington, Lancs (Tel. Penketh 2331).

Diver David Clark is used to strange sights in the depths, but even he wasn't prepared for one he came across on the English Channel bed. What was it? Turn to the next page . . .

127

NORTHUMBRIAN RIVER AUTHORITY – Rivers Controlled: Aln, Coquet, Wansbeck, Blyth, Tyne, Wear, Tees and tributaries; all other rivers entering North Sea between Goswick Sands in the north and White Stones, Boulby Cliff, nr. Staithes, Yorks, other than the Tweed and its tributaries. Licences under revision at time of going to press. Enquire from J. T. Percival, Dunira, Osborne Road, Jesmond, Newcastle-upon-Tyne 2 (Tel. Newcastle 81-2301/2/3).

SEVERN: Severn, Warwicks Avon, Teme, Vyrnwy, Banwy, Tanat; all other tributary streams in Severn watershed and canals, pools. The Severn River Authority also owns or rents water on Avon, Severn and Vyrnwy (details from Fisheries Officer). S, s. £3 3/-; for Vyrnwy and Banwy, £2 2/-; 14 d. £1 10/-, d. 7/6d.; T and FF, s. 5/-. J. D. Kelsall, Portland House, Church Street, Malvern, Worcs (Tel. Malvern 61511).

SOMERSET: Axe, Brue, Parrett and tributaries (incl. Tone, Huntspill River, King's Sedgemoor Drain, Bridgwater and Taunton Canal), Congresbury Yeo, Doniford Stream, Washford River, Avil, Horner, Hawkcombe; all reservoirs in the area. T, s. 6/6d., under 16, 3/6d.; m. 3/6d.; FF, s. 3/6d., under 16, 6d., m. 2/6d. L. Gill, The Watergate, West Quay, Bridgwater, Som. (Tel. Bridgwater 8271).

SUSSEX: Adur, Arun, Ouse, Cuckmere, all rivers in Pevensey Levels and tributaries. S and MT, s. 10/-; NT, s. 5/-; FF, s. 2/-, juv. 1/-. B. R. Thorpe, 57, Church Road, Burgess Hill, Sussex (Tel. Brighton 507101).

THAMES CONSERVANCY: River Thames between Cricklade and Teddington. Licences: nil. Permits for certain weirs, £1 per season. Fishing below Staines (Middx) is free. Above Staines are private fisheries, but some owners allow fishing. G. E. Walker, 15, Buckingham Street, Strand, W.C.2 (Tel. Trafalgar 2441).

TRENT: Trent and all tributaries; all other water within the area. S and MT, s. 10/-; NT and FF, s. 2/6d.; FF, 7 d, 1/-; under 14, free. W. F. Lester, Meadow Lane, Trent Bridge, Nottingham (Tel. Nottingham 85007).

WELLAND AND NENE: Welland and tributaries, Nene and tributaries. T and FF, 7/6d. p.a.; FF, 5/-, w. 2/-. R. E. Field, Welland and Nene River Authority, Cundle, Peterborough (Tel. Oundle 3366).

WYE: Wye, all rivers and brooks in Wye watershed, incl. Monnow, Trothy, Lugg, Arrow, Ithon, Irfon. S, s. £6 10/- (or £3 5/- in Wye above Llanwrthwl Bridge or in any tributary above Builth Bridge), 7 d. £2, 1 d. 13/-; T, s. 10/-, 7 d. 3/6d.; FF, s. 4/6d., juv. 1/-. E. M. Staite, Fishery Office, 4, St John Street, Hereford (Tel. Hereford 6313).

YORKSHIRE OUSE AND HULL: Yorkshire Ouse, its tributaries (incl. Ure, Wharfe, Nidd, Derwent, Swale, Aire, Don and Calder and tributaries); Yorkshire Esk and tributaries; Hull and tributaries, part of Humber and all tributaries of Humber from Blacktoft to Spurn Point; Hornsea Mere; all rivers flowing into sea between Spurn Point and Flamborough Head; all lakes, canals and reservoirs within the area. S and MT, Esk and tributaries and waters in the area lying to the north of the Esk; annual licence, £4, weekly £1 10/-; remainder of area, annual 5/-, weekly 2/- for S, NT and FF. M. Ll. Parry, 21, Park Square South, Leeds 1 (Tel. Leeds 29404).

NOTE: All information correct at time of going to press.

And here's the picture the diver took – just to prove he wasn't seeing things. Have YOU caught any big pandas lately?